# Kentucky Core Content Test Preparation for Reading

Grade 4

Harcourt

Orlando Austin Chicago New York Toronto London San Diego

Visit *The Learning Site!*
**www.harcourtschool.com**



Printed in the United States of America

ISBN 0-15-345905-0

2 3 4 5 6 7 8 9 10 1410 14 13 12 11 10 09

# CONTENTS

## Theme 4



## Theme 5



## Theme 6

# Tips for Taking a Test

## Preparation

1. Sit quietly.
2. Look at the speaker.
3. Listen for directions.
4. Sit straight and comfortably in your chair.
5. Keep your eyes on the teacher and the text booklet.
6. Have sharpened pencils ready.

## Mark It Correctly

**Answer choices must be marked carefully when you take a test.**

### DIRECTIONS

**Follow the directions for each item below.**

1. Mark answer choice B.
2. Mark answer choice D.
3. What letter follows C here?
4. What letter comes before D here?

### Answer Sheet

| | | | | |
|---|---|---|---|---|
| 1 | Ⓐ | Ⓑ | Ⓒ | Ⓓ |
| 2 | Ⓐ | Ⓑ | Ⓒ | Ⓓ |
| 3 | Ⓐ | Ⓑ | Ⓒ | Ⓓ |
| 4 | Ⓐ | Ⓑ | Ⓒ | Ⓓ |

# Signs Along the Way

**While you are taking a test, you should pay attention to the words and directions on the pages. Look at the words in the boxes below. Think about what you should do when you see these words on a test. Then answer the questions.**

| DIRECTIONS | GO ON | STOP | SAMPLE |
|---|---|---|---|

**1** **What word or words tell you how to do a test section?**

Ⓐ GO ON

Ⓑ DIRECTIONS

Ⓒ STOP

Ⓓ SAMPLE

**2** **What word or words tell you to continue working?**

Ⓐ GO ON

Ⓑ DIRECTIONS

Ⓒ STOP

Ⓓ SAMPLE

**3** **What word or words tell you to put your pencil down?**

Ⓐ GO ON

Ⓑ DIRECTIONS

Ⓒ STOP

Ⓓ SAMPLE

**4** **What word or words tell you that you will read an example of a particular kind of question?**

Ⓐ GO ON

Ⓑ DIRECTIONS

Ⓒ STOP

Ⓓ SAMPLE

**5** **What word or words tell you that you have reached the last question in a section?**

Ⓐ GO ON

Ⓑ DIRECTIONS

Ⓒ STOP

Ⓓ SAMPLE

# Following Directions

**When you begin a test section, read the directions carefully, paying attention to words in special type. A sample question may follow the directions. Reading it will also help you understand what you are to do.**

**Read the information in the left column. Then answer the questions about following directions.**

**DIRECTIONS**

Choose the word or group of words that means the same, or about the same, as the underlined word. Then mark the space for the answer you have chosen.

**1 The underlined word and the answer**

Ⓐ have opposite meanings

Ⓑ have similar meanings

Ⓒ do not have the same meanings

Ⓓ are the same word

**DIRECTIONS**

Read the passage. Then read each question about the passage. Decide which is the best answer to the question. Mark the space for the answer you have chosen.

**2 What should you do after you read the passage?**

Ⓐ Answer the most difficult question.

Ⓑ Reread the passage.

Ⓒ Read the questions.

Ⓓ Finish the last section.

**DIRECTIONS**

Read the sentence, paying attention to the underlined words. There may be a mistake in punctuation, capitalization, or word usage. If you find a mistake, choose the answer that is the best way to write the underlined section of the sentence. If there is no mistake, choose *Correct as is.*

**3 If you do not find an error in the sentence, which answer space should you mark?**

Ⓐ No mistake

Ⓑ Correct as is

Ⓒ DIRECTIONS

Ⓓ SAMPLE A

## Read It and Understand

**Being alert during a test means watching out for important words that will help you answer questions quickly and accurately. <u>Underlined</u> words, *italic* words, words on their own line, and words in boxes signal important information. Read the information in the left column, and answer the numbered questions on the right.**

What is the *main* reason this story was written?

**1** What is the important part of this question?

Ⓐ written

Ⓑ main

Ⓒ story

Ⓓ reason

---

Something that is <u>perplexing</u> is—

**2** What is the important part of this question?

Ⓐ Something

Ⓑ that

Ⓒ perplexing

Ⓐ is

---

Everything the colonists did angered King George *except*—

**3** What is the important part of this question?

Ⓐ King George

Ⓑ colonists

Ⓒ angered

Ⓓ except

---

Look at these guide words from a dictionary page.

almost—apple

Which word can be found on the page?

**4** What is the important part of this question?

Ⓐ almost—apple

Ⓑ Look

Ⓒ dictionary page

Ⓓ guide

Name ______________________________

*D*irections

**Read the story below. Then answer Questions 1 through 5. You may look back at the story.**

# Growing a Patch of Prairie

Kim was walking to the library when she saw her neighbor Margo in the yard. Margo was writing *For Sale* on a big piece of cardboard. On the sidewalk beside her were a lawn mower, two sprinklers, and four garden hoses.

> **Tip**
> The "For Sale" sign is probably a clue about something that happens in the story. Why might someone sell a lawn mower?

"Hi, Margo," said Kim. "It looks as if you're having a sale."

"Yes, indeed," said Margo happily. "I'm selling my lawn equipment."

"How will you take care of your lawn?" Kim asked. "Your grass is the prettiest in the neighborhood!"

"I know," said Margo. "It's green because I feed it and water it so much. I've decided that it's wrong for this area. Today, people are bringing me my new buffalo grass."

> **Tip**
> Notice that the speaker has changed. Kim speaks in the last paragraph. Margo speaks in this paragraph.

Kim thought about grass that buffaloes would eat. She imagined a little piece of the Great Plains in Margo's yard. "Are you planting a prairie?" she asked.

"Exactly!" exclaimed Margo. "This is the same grass that settlers used to build sod houses. Buffalo grass can grow without much water. Since it grows only 8 inches tall, I'll mow only a couple of times a year. I'm going to get a mower that I can power myself. Without the loud engine running, I can hear the birds."

> **Tip**
> Try to imagine what a prairie looks like. How do you think it is different from a regular lawn?

"If you're not taking care of your grass, when will I see you?" Kim asked.

Margo laughed. "Do you see those two chairs on the porch? Those chairs are for us to sit in and admire the grass. I'll have more time for relaxing than I have now."

Name ______________________________

**1 Which picture shows the setting of this story?**

A

B

C

D

**Tip**
Most of these places are mentioned in the story, but only one tells where the story happens.

**2 Margo is selling**

- **A** a big piece of cardboard
- **B** her lawn mower, sprinklers, and hoses
- **C** her yard
- **D** two chairs on her porch

**Tip**
Which answer makes sense in the story? Eliminate answers that don't make sense.

**3 Margo's lawn is so green because**

- **A** she feeds it and waters it so much
- **B** it is a new kind of grass
- **C** she doesn't mow it
- **D** she lives on the prairie

**4 According to the story, which of these statements is <u>not</u> true about buffalo grass?**

- **A** It needs to be mowed often.
- **B** Settlers used it to build sod houses.
- **C** It grows only 8 inches tall.
- **D** It needs little water.

**Tip**
Pay attention to the word *not* in the question. Which answer choice gives information that is not true?

**5 The author probably wrote this story to**

- **A** describe the best way to water a lawn
- **B** urge people to mow their lawns more often
- **C** tell people about a kind of grass that saves time and water
- **D** persuade people to buy lawn mowers



| | |
|---|---|
| 1 | Ⓐ Ⓑ Ⓒ Ⓓ |
| 2 | Ⓐ Ⓑ Ⓒ Ⓓ |
| 3 | Ⓐ Ⓑ Ⓒ Ⓓ |
| 4 | Ⓐ Ⓑ Ⓒ Ⓓ |
| 5 | Ⓐ Ⓑ Ⓒ Ⓓ |

Name ___________________________________________

# *Directions*

**Read this paragraph from a composition a student wrote about water. It has several mistakes that need correcting. Then answer Questions 6 through 8.**

### The Importance of Water

[1] Did you ever stop to think that water is necessary for all living things? [2] Plants cannot grow without water. [3] Whether they grow wild, in gardens, or on farms. [4] Animals needs water to drink. [5] people also must have water in order to live.

**6 Which statement is not a sentence?**

- **A** Statement 1
- **B** Statement 2
- **C** Statement 3
- **D** Statement 5

**Tip**
A sentence tells a complete thought. It names someone or something and tells what that person or thing is or does.

**7 Which is the best way to rewrite Sentence 4?**

- **A** An animal need water to drink.
- **B** Animals need water to drink.
- **C** Animals needing water to drink.
- **D** An animal have needed water to drink.

**Tip**
Remember that the verb must agree with its subject.

**8 How should the error in Sentence 5 be corrected?**

- **A** by changing the period to a question mark
- **B** by capitalizing the first word of the sentence
- **C** by adding a comma after *also*
- **D** by writing it without an end mark



| | |
|---|---|
| 6 | Ⓐ Ⓑ Ⓒ Ⓓ |
| 7 | Ⓐ Ⓑ Ⓒ Ⓓ |
| 8 | Ⓐ Ⓑ Ⓒ Ⓓ |

Name ______________________________

## *Directions*

**Look at the underlined part of the sentence. Choose the answer that shows the correct punctuation for that part. If the underlined part is correct, mark "Correct as is."**

**9 The house on the corner. has a beautiful green lawn.**

A corner has

B corner? has

C corner, has

D Correct as is

**Tip**
First identify a punctuation error in the underlined part of the sentence. Then decide how to correct it.

**10 Read the phrases. Look for an underlined word that contains a usage error. If the underlined words are used correctly, mark "All correct."**

A days of the weak

B ties a shoe

C running fast

D All correct

**11 Choose the word that is spelled correctly and completes the sentence.**

**I enjoy working outdoors with others in my ______.**

A famly

B fammily

C famelly

D family

**12 Write two complete sentences about a good neighbor. Capitalize and punctuate correctly.**

______________________________

______________________________

______________________________

**Tip**
Check each of your sentences to be sure it expresses a complete thought.



| | |
|---|---|
| 9 | Ⓐ Ⓑ Ⓒ Ⓓ |
| 10 | Ⓐ Ⓑ Ⓒ Ⓓ |
| 11 | Ⓐ Ⓑ Ⓒ Ⓓ |

STOP

Name ________________________________

*D*irections

**Read the poem below. Then answer Questions 1 through 5. You may look back at the poem.**

# On the Interstate

Driving down the interstate,
Hoping that we will not be late,
We come to an interchange,
A place where routes may rearrange
Because two highways intersect.
In other words, they interconnect.
Mom says, "Go left." Dad says, "Go right."
We wait an interminable time at the light.
The light was red, but now it's green.
I don't interfere or intervene.
They reach an agreement. They make a decision.
Will we get to the show before intermission?

**Tip**
As you read the poem, ask yourself questions. Who is the narrator? Why is it important not to be late?

**Tip**
Have you noticed that many of the words in this poem have the prefix *inter-* ? Look for other prefixes, suffixes, and root words that you know.

Name ____________________

1 **Which of these words means "not seeming to end" and has the prefix *in-*, meaning "not"?**

A interchange

B intersect

C interminable

D interconnect

**Tip**
Three of the words have the prefix *inter-*, meaning "between." Figure out the meanings of the answer choices by looking back at the poem to see how they are used.

2 **Who is the narrator of the poem?**

A the driver of the car

B a child riding in the family car

C Dad

D a highway patrol officer

**Tip**
The narrator does not directly identify himself or herself, but you can draw a conclusion from clues in the poem.

3 **Where are the people in the car going?**

A to a show

B home

C to a restaurant

D The poem does not say.

4 **What word best describes the tone of this poem?**

A serious

B angry

C playful

D uninterested

**Tip**
Choose the answer that best describes the feeling the author conveys by the choice of words and the way the poem is written.

5 **Notice the rhyming pattern in the poem. Write a poem of four lines with the same pattern.**

____________________

____________________

____________________

____________________



| | |
|---|---|
| 1 | Ⓐ Ⓑ Ⓒ Ⓓ |
| 2 | Ⓐ Ⓑ Ⓒ Ⓓ |
| 3 | Ⓐ Ⓑ Ⓒ Ⓓ |
| 4 | Ⓐ Ⓑ Ⓒ Ⓓ |

Name ___________________________________________

# *Directions*

**Read this paragraph from a composition a student wrote. It has several mistakes that need correcting. Then answer Questions 6 through 8.**

**Jeff's Bird Feeder**

[1] Jeff wanted to make a bird feeder. [2] His friend meg tells him how to make a feeder from an empty plastic soda bottle. [3] When the feeder was done, Dad gave Jeff seeds to put in it. [4] helped Jeff hang the feeder from the branch of a tree. [5] Now Jeff enjoys watching from the window as the birds eat from his feeder.

**6 How can the error in Statement 4 be corrected?**

**A** by changing the period to a question mark

**B** by changing the small *h* in *helped* to a capital *H*

**C** by adding the subject *He* before *helped*

**D** by adding a comma after *feeder*

> **Tip**
> As you read each answer choice, look back at Statement 4 to decide whether or not the sentence would be correct after making this change.

**7 Which is the best way to rewrite Sentence 2?**

**A** His friend meg told him how to make a feeder from an empty plastic soda bottle.

**B** His friend Meg tells him how to make a feeder from an empty plastic soda bottle.

**C** His friend Meg told him how to make a feeder from an empty plastic soda bottle.

**D** His friend meg tells him how to make a feeder from an empty plastic soda bottle?

> **Tip**
> Look carefully at Sentence 2. You may find that there is more than one error that needs to be corrected.

**8 Which of these statements is true about Sentence 5?**

**A** It is written in the present tense.

**B** It is written in the past tense.

**C** It is an interrogative sentence.

**D** It is a sentence fragment.



6 Ⓐ Ⓑ Ⓒ Ⓓ
7 Ⓐ Ⓑ Ⓒ Ⓓ
8 Ⓐ Ⓑ Ⓒ Ⓓ

Name ____________________

*Directions*

**Look at the underlined part of the sentence. Choose the answer that shows the correct punctuation for that part. If the underlined part is correct, mark "Correct as is."**

**9 Did you see that bright red bird.**

**A** bird
**B** bird?
**C** bird,
**D** Correct as is

**Tip**
Think about what end mark is correct for this type of sentence.

**10 Read the sentence. Choose the answer that tells which word should be capitalized. If the capitalization is correct, mark "Correct as is."**

**Mr. henry drove his truck from the city to the lake.**

**A** henry
**B** city
**C** lake
**D** Correct as is

**Tip**
Decide whether each choice is a common noun or a proper noun. Proper nouns should be capitalized.

**11 Read the phrases. Choose the phrase containing an underlined word that is spelled wrong. If all the underlined words are spelled correctly, mark "All correct."**

**A** a loud screem
**B** a good reason
**C** a flock of geese
**D** All correct

**12 Write a declarative sentence and an interrogative sentence about a long trip by car. Capitalize and punctuate correctly.**

____________________

____________________

____________________

____________________

____________________

| | |
|---|---|
| 9 | Ⓐ Ⓑ Ⓒ Ⓓ |
| 10 | Ⓐ Ⓑ Ⓒ Ⓓ |
| 11 | Ⓐ Ⓑ Ⓒ Ⓓ |

STOP

Name ______________________________

*Directions*

**Read the story below. Then answer Questions 1 through 5. You may look back at the story.**

# A Work of Art

Our project started with a notice in the school paper about a school art fair. "I want everyone to bring in something for the fair," our teacher said. "You can work in pairs if you like."

Soon everyone else was working on their projects. Only Isaac and I had no ideas. We decided to try our school library. Candlemaking? Flower arranging? Origami? None of these interested us. Then, near the end of the art section, we saw it.

"Hey, Wally, what do you think of these pictures?" Isaac asked me. The cover of the book showed a dressed-up dog. The photographs were by William Wegman.

"These are cool!" I said. So Isaac and I decided to be animal photographers. We planned our project and had some wonderful ideas. We would put Samson in a hat and get him to sit still while we took his picture.

**Tip**
In this sentence, the word *cool* is used as slang. It does not have its usual meaning, "slightly cold." Authors sometimes use slang in dialogue to make their characters' speech seem more realistic.

Isaac came over the next afternoon. We borrowed a beret from my sister.

**Tip**
If you don't know what the word *beret* means, read on to see if there is something later in the story that can help you figure out the meaning.

"This will look great!" Isaac said.

Well, Samson didn't think so. He shook the hat off his head right away. We decided to try the sombrero my parents got in Mexico. When I tied the string under his chin, the hat covered Samson's eyes. He shook his head back and forth and made funny noises. My mother told us to leave him alone.

"Why don't you two boys walk around the neighborhood and take some pictures?" she suggested.

So that's what we did. Our pictures weren't the most exciting ones in the art fair. They didn't win any prizes, but at least Samson enjoyed the rest of his day.

Name ______________________________

1 **The problem faced by the main character in this story is**

**A** finding a partner to work with

**B** planning and completing an art project

**C** finding a hat for Samson

**D** a disagreement with his mother

> **Tip**
> To answer this question, first identify the main character. Then identify the problem this character has to solve.

2 **Here are some events from the story. Place the events in order from 1 to 4 by writing the numbers in the boxes next to each sentence.**

☐ The boys enter pictures at the art fair.

☐ The boys walk around the neighborhood.

☐ The boys go to the library.

☐ The boys try to take pictures of Samson.

> **Tip**
> If you are not sure of the order of events, don't guess. Look back at the story.

3 **Samson is probably**

**A** Wally's sister

**B** a classmate

**C** a dog

**D** a visitor from Mexico

> **Tip**
> The story does not tell who or what Samson is. However, you can use clues from the story, such as how the boys decide on their project and how Samson behaves, to figure out his identity.

4 **The meaning of the word *beret* in this story is**

**A** a hat

**B** a scarf

**C** a head

**D** a string

5 **Samson enjoyed the rest of his day because**

**A** he had a new hat to wear

**B** the boys took his picture

**C** he got to go for a walk

**D** no one was trying to dress him up



| | |
|---|---|
| 1 | Ⓐ Ⓑ Ⓒ Ⓓ |
| 3 | Ⓐ Ⓑ Ⓒ Ⓓ |
| 4 | Ⓐ Ⓑ Ⓒ Ⓓ |
| 5 | Ⓐ Ⓑ Ⓒ Ⓓ |

Name ______________________________

## *Directions*

**Read these paragraphs from a composition a student wrote about a friend. There are several mistakes that need correcting. Then answer Questions 6 through 8.**

**My Friend Rita**

1 Rita is good at drawing. 2 Rita is good at painting.

3 What fantastic work she does? 4 She say, "I want to be an artist when I grow up."

5 I say, "Rita, you are an artist already!"

**6 Choose the BEST way to combine Sentences 1 and 2.**

**A** Rita is good at drawing, Rita is good at painting.
**B** Rita is good at drawing, and Rita is good at painting.
**C** Rita is good at drawing and painting.
**D** Rita are good at drawing and painting.

**Tip**
Eliminate choices that have errors in punctuation or usage. From the remaining sentences, choose the one that avoids repeating words that do not need to be repeated.

**7 Sentence 3 should end with ______ instead of a question mark.**

**A** a period
**B** a comma
**C** a semicolon
**D** an exclamation point

**Tip**
Reread Sentence 3 to decide what type of sentence it is. Choose the end mark that is correct for this type of sentence.

**8 How can the error in Sentence 4 be corrected?**

**A** by changing *say* to *says*
**B** by changing *want* to *wants*
**C** by changing *an* to *a*
**D** by changing the period to a question mark

| | |
|---|---|
| 6 | Ⓐ Ⓑ Ⓒ Ⓓ |
| 7 | Ⓐ Ⓑ Ⓒ Ⓓ |
| 8 | Ⓐ Ⓑ Ⓒ Ⓓ |

Name ________________________________________

## Directions

**Read the sentence. Choose the answer that shows which words in the sentence should be capitalized. If the capitalization is correct, mark "Correct as is."**

**9 My brother ed and i go to the same school.**

**A** My brother ed and I go to the same school.
**B** My brother Ed and I go to the same school.
**C** My Brother Ed and I go to the same School.
**D** Correct as is

**10 Which of the following is a compound word?**

**A** unfriendly
**B** useful
**C** uphill
**D** umbrella

> **Tip**
> Remember that a compound word is made up of two smaller words. Don't confuse compound words with root words that have prefixes or suffixes added.

**11 Choose the word that is spelled correctly and completes the sentence.**

**Everyone _______ to the window to see what was happening.**

**A** hurryed
**B** hurried
**C** hurreyd
**D** hurreied

> **Tip**
> First think of how to spell the root word. Then recall how the spelling changes when the *-ed* ending is added.

**12 Write an imperative sentence and an exclamatory sentence that you might hear at an art show. Capitalize and punctuate correctly.**

________________________________________

________________________________________

________________________________________

________________________________________



| | |
|---|---|
| 9 | Ⓐ Ⓑ Ⓒ Ⓓ |
| 10 | Ⓐ Ⓑ Ⓒ Ⓓ |
| 11 | Ⓐ Ⓑ Ⓒ Ⓓ |

STOP

Name ______________________________

*Directions*

**Read the article below. Then answer Questions 1 through 5. You may look back at the article.**

# A New Sport

Do you like to get out in the country and visit with nature? Do you like to ride a bike? If so, you should try racing in an event called cyclocross. In this sport, you have to ride your bike, *and* you have to carry it!

> **Tip**
> Look carefully at the word *cyclocross*. Use the meanings of the word parts to form an idea of what this sport is.

You spend only part of the race on your bike because only half of the course is smooth. The other half goes through country fields. Bikers travel through areas filled with logs, sandpits, mud puddles, fences, and piles of wood. Several times during the race, riders hop off their bikes, hang them over their shoulders, and run as fast as they can while carrying the bikes.

> **Tip**
> Don't stop reading to memorize details. Read the whole passage to understand the main ideas. You can look back at the passage later if you need to recall details to answer questions.

Deciding when to ride and when to run is part of a racer's strategy. At some points, however, barricades or hurdles are set up to force riders to get off their bikes. These barricades are from 10 to 15 inches high and set close together. While running with their bikes on their shoulders, the racers also have to jump over the barricades. As you can imagine, you must be a strong athlete with good skills to compete in this sport!

Cyclocross began in Europe about ten years ago as a way for cyclists to stay fit during the winter. The sport helps bike riders develop their skills, strength, and endurance.

A cyclocross race usually takes one hour from start to finish. If you work out an hour a day, three or four days a week, you'll probably be strong enough to compete in one. You will need to do some uphill running and exercises that build muscles in your lower back, stomach, and legs. Check out sports magazines or do a computer search for more information about cyclocross. It's a great way to see the countryside while having fun.

> **Tip**
> Most of the article gives information about the sport itself. In this last paragraph, the focus changes. This paragraph gives advice about how a person might train for the sport.

Name ______________________________

1 **What meaning of the root word *cross* is combined with *cyclo* to form the name of the sport?**

**A** bad-tempered

**B** to meet and pass on the way

**C** to draw a line through something

**D** to move across or over a distance

> **Tip**
> Try putting together the meanings for *cross* with *cycle* or *bicycle* to see which meaning best describes the sport.

2 **Why is this article called "A New Sport"?**

**A** because bicycles are a new invention

**B** because cyclocross is completely different from other sports

**C** because cyclocross began about ten years ago

**D** because cyclocross races last for about an hour

> **Tip**
> Read the answer choices carefully. Watch out for the word *completely.*

3 **Which picture shows an obstacle you would probably not come upon in a cyclocross race?**

**A**

**B**

**C**

**D**

4 **Which statement is an opinion about cyclocross?**

**A** The sport began in Europe.

**B** Cyclocross is a great way to see the countryside.

**C** Riders carry their bikes on their shoulders.

**D** Barricades may be 10 to 15 inches high.

5 **Which of these headings best states the main idea of the last paragraph of the article?**

**A** More Facts About Cyclocross

**B** Exercises for Fun and Fitness

**C** Getting Ready for Cyclocross

**D** How to See the Countryside

| | |
|---|---|
| 1 | Ⓐ Ⓑ Ⓒ Ⓓ |
| 2 | Ⓐ Ⓑ Ⓒ Ⓓ |
| 3 | Ⓐ Ⓑ Ⓒ Ⓓ |
| 4 | Ⓐ Ⓑ Ⓒ Ⓓ |
| 5 | Ⓐ Ⓑ Ⓒ Ⓓ |

Name ______________________________

## *Directions*

**Read this paragraph. Then answer questions 6 through 8.**

> [1] Henry Aaron was born in Alabama in 1934, the same year that the great Babe Ruth ended his baseball career with the New York Yankees. [2] Babe Ruth had hit 714 home runs, a record that stood for forty years. [3] It was Henry Aaron who broke that record when he hit home run number 715 on April 8, 1974. [4] Aaron also holds the major league record for runs batted in.

**6 Which sentence below would be the best closing sentence for the paragraph?**

**A** Babe Ruth was a great baseball player.

**B** Baseball is a popular sport in other parts of the world, as well as in the United States.

**C** In 1982, Henry Aaron was elected to the National Baseball Hall of Fame.

**D** A home run usually means that the batter hits the ball over the fence and out of the ballpark.

**Tip**
Think about the main idea of the paragraph and how the text is structured. Pick the answer that tells more about the main idea and fits the structure of the paragraph.

**7 The pronoun *his* in the first sentence refers to**

**A** Babe Ruth

**B** Henry Aaron

**C** the New York Yankees

**D** the author of the paragraph

**8 Where would this sentence best fit in the paragraph?**

**He went on to hit a total of 755 home runs.**

**A** before Sentence 1

**B** before Sentence 2

**C** before Sentence 3

**D** before Sentence 4

**Tip**
Try rereading the paragraph with the new sentence in each position. Think about where the sentence fits best into the sequence of events.



| | |
|---|---|
| 6 | Ⓐ Ⓑ Ⓒ Ⓓ |
| 7 | Ⓐ Ⓑ Ⓒ Ⓓ |
| 8 | Ⓐ Ⓑ Ⓒ Ⓓ |

Name ____________________

*Directions*

**Read the sentence. Choose the answer that tells the predicate of the sentence.**

**9 My sister plays first base on her Little League team.**

**A** my sister

**B** my sister plays first base

**C** plays first base on her Little League team

**D** on her Little League team

> **Tip**
> First identify the subject, which names the person or thing that the sentence is about. The predicate tells what the subject of the sentence is or does.

**10 Read the phrases. Look for an underlined word that contains a usage error. If the underlined words are used correctly, mark "All correct."**

**A** over there

**B** in it's place

**C** a new bicycle

**D** All correct

**11 Choose the word that is spelled correctly and completes the sentence.**

**We often ask our friends to eat ______ with us.**

**A** diner

**B** dinor

**C** dinner

**D** dinnar

**12 Write a sentence about a sport or outdoor activity that you enjoy. Draw one line under the subject of the sentence. Draw two lines under the predicate. Capitalize and punctuate correctly.**

_______________________________________________

_______________________________________________

_______________________________________________



| | |
|---|---|
| 9 | Ⓐ Ⓑ Ⓒ Ⓓ |
| 10 | Ⓐ Ⓑ Ⓒ Ⓓ |
| 11 | Ⓐ Ⓑ Ⓒ Ⓓ |

STOP

Name ______________________________

*D*irections

**Read the article below. Then answer Questions 1 through 5. You may look back at the article.**

# Unstoppable Clara Barton

Clara Barton was born in 1821 in Massachusetts. She was always a bright and independent child, though somewhat shy. As she grew older, she discovered that she enjoyed nursing the sick and helping people in need.

## The Civil War

In 1861, when the Civil War broke out, Clara Barton went to work helping wounded soldiers. She had to make nutritious food from limited supplies, comfort the patients, make sure they had water, and assist the surgeons in dangerous battlefield conditions. Clara did it all, and she did it well.

After the Civil War ended, Clara Barton gave public talks about her experiences. This was a time before movies, radio, or television. One form of entertainment was to go to a public hall to hear someone speak about interesting events. Clara's talks were popular. Before long, her heroism and hard work on the battlefields became known throughout the country.

## The Red Cross

In 1869, while visiting Switzerland, Clara Barton learned about the Red Cross. She set out to start an American branch of this organization that helped people in times of war and disaster. In 1881, as a result of her efforts, the American Red Cross became a reality.

Clara Barton headed the American Red Cross until she was 82. Monuments honoring her war work and her life of service can be seen at Antietam National Battlefield and at her final home in Glen Echo, Maryland.

**Tip**
Notice the headings that divide the article into sections. These headings tell what each section is about. They can help you locate information when you look back at the article.

**Tip**
Notice words like *after* and *before* that signal the order of events.

Name ______________________________

1 **This article can <u>best</u> be described as**

A an informational article about the Red Cross

B historical fiction

C a brief biography

D an advertisement for the Red Cross

2 **Why does the title of the article call Clara Barton unstoppable?**

A because she was shy as a child

B because she worked in dangerous conditions

C because she lived a long time

D because she was determined and did what she set out to do

**Tip**
Notice the prefix, root word, and suffix in the word *unstoppable.* Think about the meaning of the word and how it applies to what the author tells you about Clara Barton.

3 **The article gives enough information for you to conclude that Clara Barton**

A enjoyed public speaking more than she enjoyed helping others

B loved to travel

C was deeply affected by her experiences during the Civil War

D was sorry for many of her actions

4 **Which part of a textbook would be most helpful for locating information about the Antietam National Battlefield?**

A the title

B the index

C the chapter headings

D the glossary

5 **Write a sentence that tells the author's purpose for writing this article.**

______________________________

______________________________

______________________________

| | |
|---|---|
| 1 | Ⓐ Ⓑ Ⓒ Ⓓ |
| 2 | Ⓐ Ⓑ Ⓒ Ⓓ |
| 3 | Ⓐ Ⓑ Ⓒ Ⓓ |
| 4 | Ⓐ Ⓑ Ⓒ Ⓓ |





GO ON

Name ______________________________

## *Directions*

**Look at this part of an index from a book about Amelia Earhart. Then answer questions 6 through 8.**

**Index**



**6 Using the index above, where would you look to find information about Amelia Earhart's part in the development of commercial airlines?**

**A** Airline industry, role in

**B** Early career

**C** First flight from Hawaii to California

**D** Flight across Atlantic Ocean

> **Tip**
> Identify one or more specific key words in your topic to look up in the index. Remember that topics are listed in alphabetical order.

**7 On which pages would you look to find out how Amelia Earhart first became a pilot?**

**A** pp. 19, 26

**B** pp. 5–16

**C** pp. 31–49

**D** pp. 17–30

> **Tip**
> To answer this question, first decide what topic listed in the index best matches the information you want. Then look at the page numbers listed for that topic.

**8 Where should the topic *Childhood* be added to this table of contents?**

**A** before *Airline industry, role in*

**B** between *Airline industry, role in* and *Early Career*

**C** between *Early Career* and *First flight from Hawaii to California*

**D** after *Flight across Atlantic Ocean*



| | |
|---|---|
| **6** | Ⓐ Ⓑ Ⓒ Ⓓ |
| **7** | Ⓐ Ⓑ Ⓒ Ⓓ |
| **8** | Ⓐ Ⓑ Ⓒ Ⓓ |

Name ________________________________________

## *Directions*

**Look at the underlined part of the sentence. Choose the answer that shows the correct punctuation for that part. If the underlined part is correct, mark "Correct as is."**

> **Tip**
> Can you identify more than one complete thought? Decide whether the example is a run-on sentence that should be written as two separate sentences.

**9 We thought we were lost in the woods we used a compass to find our way.**

- **A** woods, we
- **B** woods. We
- **C** woods. we
- **D** Correct as is

> **Tip**
> Notice that *fine* is used as a noun in the sentence. Eliminate phrases in which *fine* is not used as a noun.

**10 Read the sentence. Then choose the answer in which the word *fine* has the same meaning as it does in the sentence.**

**When the time on the parking meter expired, I had to pay a fine.**

- **A** feeling fine
- **B** reading fine print
- **C** fine weather
- **D** a fine for overdue books

**11 Read the phrases. Choose the phrase containing an underlined word that is spelled wrong. If all the underlined words are spelled correctly, mark "All correct."**

- **A** a red balloon
- **B** a large group
- **C** a bowl of fruit
- **D** All correct

**12 Write a sentence about a person you admire. Draw one line under the complete subject of the sentence. Draw a circle around the simple subject. Capitalize and punctuate correctly.**

________________________________________

________________________________________

________________________________________

| | |
|---|---|
| 9 | Ⓐ Ⓑ Ⓒ Ⓓ |
| 10 | Ⓐ Ⓑ Ⓒ Ⓓ |
| 11 | Ⓐ Ⓑ Ⓒ Ⓓ |

STOP

Name ______________________________

## *Directions*

**WRITE A PERSONAL EXPERIENCE NARRATIVE** **Think about a time when you were proud of something that you accomplished. Write a narrative about the experience. Include details about the events leading up to the accomplishment.**

**Use the story map below to plan your narrative, and write it on a separate sheet of paper. When you are finished with the draft, use the Writer's Checklist to revise and edit your work. Then make a final copy of your narrative.**

**Characters**

**Setting**

**Beginning**

**Middle**

**Ending**

Name ______________________________

## *Writer's Checklist*

- ❑ Does your narrative have a clear beginning, middle, and ending?
- ❑ Did you tell the story in your own voice, using the pronoun *I*?
- ❑ Did you tell about the events leading up to the accomplishment?
- ❑ Did you include interesting words and details?
- ❑ Did you organize your narrative in paragraphs?
- ❑ Did you include different types of sentences?
- ❑ Do you have any run-on sentences or fragments?
- ❑ Did you begin sentences and names of people with capital letters?
- ❑ Did you end every sentence with an end mark?
- ❑ Did you try to spell each word correctly?



STOP

Name ______________________________

*Directions*

**Read the play below. Then answer Questions 1 through 5. You may look back at the play.**

# The Smell of Soup

A Tale from Turkey

CHARACTERS

Poor Man — Innkeeper

Hodja, *a judge* — Villagers

**SETTING:** *A courtyard in an old town.*

**AT RISE:** *The innkeeper is standing in the doorway of his inn. A poor man dressed in rags approaches.*

**POOR MAN:** Good morning. Can you spare me some soup?

**INNKEEPER:** (*Impatiently.*) No, I cannot. (*He goes inside.*)

**POOR MAN:** (*Calling after him.*) Good day then, and may you be well. (*He starts to walk away, then stops and sniffs.*) I smell something cooking. My, it smells good.

**INNKEEPER:** (*Rushing out.*) Did you steal some of my soup?

**POOR MAN:** No, sir. I was only smelling the delicious aroma.

**INNKEEPER:** Then you must pay for the smell! (*To villagers.*) Call the judge! (*A villager leaves and returns with Hodja.*)

**HODJA:** What is your complaint, Innkeeper?

**INNKEEPER:** Hodja, I caught this man smelling my soup!

**HODJA:** So you want to be paid for the smell of your soup? (*Innkeeper nods eagerly.*) I shall pay you myself. (*He takes two gold coins from his pocket and strikes them together to make a loud ringing sound.*) I have paid for the smell of your soup with the sound of my money. Now please be on your way. (*Villagers cheer.*)

**Tip**
Stage directions are in parentheses and printed in slanted type. They help you understand the actions of the play by telling how characters speak and what they do.

**Tip**
As you read, think about the reasons why events happen. Why does the poor man stop and sniff? Read on to find the cause for his action.

**Tip**
If you do not remember who *Hodja* is, look back at the list of characters at the beginning of the play.

Name ________________________________

**1 The AT RISE section tells you**

**A** who the characters are

**B** who is speaking

**C** what is happening as the play begins

**D** where the play takes place

> **Tip**
> If you don't recall the purpose of the AT RISE section, go back and reread it.

**2 Which word is a synonym for *aroma*?**

**A** smell

**B** soup

**C** sniff

**D** money

> **Tip**
> If this word is not familiar, look back at the play to see how it is used. The context can help you understand its meaning.

**3 Which word best describes the innkeeper in this play?**

**A** greedy

**B** honest

**C** unintelligent

**D** cheerful

**4 The two things that Hodja compares are**

**A** the sound of eating soup with the sound of money clinking together

**B** the smell of soup cooking with the sound of coins clinking together

**C** the smell of soup cooking with the taste of soup

**D** the sound of coins with the sound of the villagers cheering

> **Tip**
> Read each answer choice carefully. Some of them are very similar. Be sure that both parts of the answer are correct before you mark your answer.

**5 Early in the play, why does the poor man stop and sniff?**

________________________________

________________________________



| | |
|---|---|
| 1 | Ⓐ Ⓑ Ⓒ Ⓓ |
| 2 | Ⓐ Ⓑ Ⓒ Ⓓ |
| 3 | Ⓐ Ⓑ Ⓒ Ⓓ |
| 4 | Ⓐ Ⓑ Ⓒ Ⓓ |

Name ______________________________

# *Directions*

**Read this story that a student wrote. It has several mistakes that need correcting. Then answer Questions 6 through 8.**

**Storm Cookies**

[1] One stormy night, Antonio and Maya were making cookies. [2] They had just finished mixing the cookie dough suddenly the lights went out. [3] Without electricity, they cannot bake their cookies.

[4] "Oh well," said Maya. [5] "That's the way the cookie crumbles."

**Tip**
Look for a run-on sentence that contains a subject and predicate that express one complete thought, and another subject and predicate that express a different complete thought.

**6 Which sentence contains two complete thoughts and should be written as two sentences?**

**A** Sentence 1
**B** Sentence 2
**C** Sentence 3
**D** Sentence 4

**Tip**
Verb tenses show whether events are told about in the past, present, or future. Pick the tense that fits the rest of the story.

**7 Which is the best way to rewrite Sentence 3?**

**A** Without electricity, they can't bake their cookies.
**B** Without electricity, they will not bake their cookies.
**C** Without electricity, they could not bake their cookies.
**D** Without electricity, they are not baking their cookies.

**8 How else could Sentence 5 be written and still be correct?**

**A** "That's the way the cookie crumbles".
**B** "That's the way the cookie crumbles!"
**C** "That's the way the cookie crumbles,"
**D** "That's the way the cookie crumbles?"



6 Ⓐ Ⓑ Ⓒ Ⓓ
7 Ⓐ Ⓑ Ⓒ Ⓓ
8 Ⓐ Ⓑ Ⓒ Ⓓ

Name ____________________

## *Directions*

**Read the sentence. Choose the answer that shows which word in the sentence should be capitalized. If the capitalization is correct, mark "Correct as is."**

**9 The cook at the Fireside restaurant makes great vegetable soup.**

**A** cook
**B** restaurant
**C** vegetable
**D** Correct as is

> **Tip**
> Remember that a proper noun names a particular person, place, or thing. Each important word of a proper noun should begin with a capital letter.

**10 Choose the word or words that correctly complete the sentence.**

**Now I ______ helping my parents in the kitchen.**

**A** enjoys
**B** enjoying
**C** enjoy
**D** has enjoyed

**11 Choose the word that is spelled correctly and completes the sentence.**

**A ______ uses tools such as a hammer and nails.**

**A** carpenter
**B** carpinter
**C** carrpenter
**D** carepenter

**12 Write a sentence about your favorite food. Draw one line under the complete predicate. Draw a circle around the simple predicate. Capitalize and punctuate correctly.**

> **Tip**
> The complete predicate tells what the subject of the sentence is or does. The simple predicate is the main word or words in the complete predicate.

______________________________________________

______________________________________________

______________________________________________

| | |
|---|---|
| 9 | Ⓐ Ⓑ Ⓒ Ⓓ |
| 10 | Ⓐ Ⓑ Ⓒ Ⓓ |
| 11 | Ⓐ Ⓑ Ⓒ Ⓓ |

STOP

Name ____________________

*Directions*

**Read the folktale below. Then answer Questions 1 through 5. You may look back at the story.**

# The Golden Reed Pipe

## A Folktale from China

Long ago in China, there lived a woman and her daughter. The daughter was called Little Red because she loved red clothing. One day, a dragon swooped down and carried Little Red away. Her mother heard Little Red's voice crying:

*Oh mother, oh mother, as dear as can be.*
*My brother, my brother will rescue me!*

The poor mother did not know what to think, as she had no son. Then one day she found a lost little boy under a bright red berry plant. She named him Redberry.

Redberry was outside when he heard a crow cry:

*You have a sister out there, out there!*
*Save her from the dragon's lair!*

Redberry ran to his mother, who told him about Little Red and what had happened. So the boy set out to rescue his sister. He walked until he came to a large rock. He rolled the rock away and found a golden reed pipe.

**Tip**
The title of the story is "The Golden Reed Pipe." From this, you can draw the conclusion that the golden reed pipe Redberry finds is probably going to be important in the story.

When Redberry blew on the pipe, all the frogs and other creatures began to dance. The faster the tune, the faster they danced. "Aha!" cried Redberry. "Now I can deal with the dragon!"

**Tip**
How do you think Redberry plans to deal with the dragon? Read the rest of the story to confirm your prediction.

When he came to the dragon's cave, he saw a girl dressed in red. Redberry blew on the pipe, and the dragon began to dance. The faster Redberry played, the faster the dragon danced. At last the dragon cried:

*I'll send her home*
*If you leave me alone!*

Redberry knew better than to believe a dragon. He kept on playing until they came to the sea. With a splash, the dragon fell in! Then the sister and brother returned home to their mother, who smiled with joy to see them.

Name ______________________________

1 **Because the story is a folktale, you know that it**

**A** is based on real events
**B** was first told orally
**C** was made up and written down by the same person
**D** gives information about a topic

2 **Here are some events from the story. Place the events in order from 1 to 4 by writing the numbers in the boxes next to each sentence.**

☐ Little Red's mother finds Redberry.
☐ Redberry moves the rock.
☐ Redberry sees the dragon.
☐ Little Red says her brother will rescue her.

**Tip**
Remember that you can look back at the story to help you recall details such as the order of events.

3 **Before the crow speaks to him, Redberry does not know**

**A** how to play a reed pipe
**B** who his mother is
**C** that he has a sister
**D** that crows can talk

**Tip**
To find the answer to this question, skim the story to find the part where the crow speaks to Redberry.

4 **When Redberry sees the frogs and other creatures dancing, he gets the idea**

**A** to keep the animals as pets
**B** to entertain the dragon with his music
**C** to make his living playing the golden reed pipe
**D** to make the dragon dance and not let him stop

5 **If the plot changed so that Redberry played an electric guitar instead of a pipe, how else would the story change?**

**A** It would be set in a different time.
**B** Little Red would not be rescued.
**C** Redberry could be timid instead of brave.
**D** There would not be a dragon in the story.

**Tip**
Try to imagine the story with the same characters, setting, and plot, but with an electric guitar instead of a pipe. What other part of the story no longer makes sense as a result of this change?

| | |
|---|---|
| 1 | Ⓐ Ⓑ Ⓒ Ⓓ |
| 3 | Ⓐ Ⓑ Ⓒ Ⓓ |
| 4 | Ⓐ Ⓑ Ⓒ Ⓓ |
| 5 | Ⓐ Ⓑ Ⓒ Ⓓ |





GO ON

Name ______________________________

*Directions*

**Read this retelling of a familiar fable. It has several mistakes that need correcting. Then answer Questions 6 through 8.**

**The Lion And The Mouse**

[1]A lion was fast asleep under a tree. [2]A little mouse ran across the lion's face. [3] The lion woke up and roared in anger. [4] Grabbed the mouse in his huge paw. [5] The mouse begged the lion to set him free and promised to return the favor some day. [6] The mouse gnawed through the ropes and saved the lion.

**6 Which statement is not a complete sentence because it has no subject?**

**A** Statement 1

**B** Statement 2

**C** Statement 4

**D** Statement 6

> **Tip**
> Remember that the subject of a sentence tells who or what the sentence is about. Look for a statement that tells what someone does but does not tell who does it.

**7 What is the correct way to capitalize the title? If the title is written correctly, mark "Correct as is."**

**A** The lion and the mouse

**B** the Lion and the Mouse

**C** The Lion and the Mouse

**D** Correct as is

**8 Where would this sentence <u>best</u> fit in the paragraph?**

**Then one day the lion got caught in a trap made of ropes.**

**A** after Sentence 2

**B** after Sentence 3

**C** after Sentence 4

**D** after Sentence 5

> **Tip**
> Think about the sequence of events in the story and where this event makes sense in that sequence.



| | |
|---|---|
| 6 | Ⓐ Ⓑ Ⓒ Ⓓ |
| 7 | Ⓐ Ⓑ Ⓒ Ⓓ |
| 8 | Ⓐ Ⓑ Ⓒ Ⓓ |

Name ______________________________

# Directions

**Look at the underlined part of the sentence. Choose the answer that shows the correct punctuation for that part. If the underlined part is correct, mark "Correct as is."**

**9 Frogs, worms, and, snakes danced to the music.**

**A** Frogs worms and snakes
**B** Frogs, worms, and snakes
**C** Frogs worms, and snakes
**D** Correct as is

**Tip**
Notice that the sentence has a compound subject. Think about the correct way to use commas in a compound subject.

**10 Read the phrases. Look for an underlined word that contains a usage error. If the underlined words are used correctly, mark "All correct."**

**A** a good job
**B** the bestest player
**C** most amazing of all
**D** All correct

**11 Read the phrases. Choose the phrase containing an underlined word that is spelled wrong. If all the underlined words are spelled correctly, mark "All correct."**

**A** a young child
**B** heading north
**C** make a promiss
**D** All correct

**12 Write two sentences about music. Write the first sentence with a compound subject, and the second with a compound predicate. Capitalize and punctuate correctly.**

______________________________

______________________________

______________________________

______________________________

**Tip**
For your compound subject, use two or more subjects joined by *and* or *or*. For your compound predicate, use two or more predicates joined by *and* or *or*.

| | |
|---|---|
| **9** | Ⓐ Ⓑ Ⓒ Ⓓ |
| **10** | Ⓐ Ⓑ Ⓒ Ⓓ |
| **11** | Ⓐ Ⓑ Ⓒ Ⓓ |

STOP

Name ___________________________________________

*Directions*

**Read the article below. Then answer Questions 1 through 5. You may look back at the article.**

# A Land of Fire and Ice

Would you like to visit a land where you can see things that are both very hot and very cold? Iceland is a country that has both volcanoes and glaciers. That is why the country is called the "Land of Fire and Ice."

**Tip**
Pay close attention to parts of the article that explain the title. Often you will be asked questions about titles.

Iceland, about the same size as the state of Virginia, has more hot springs and volcanoes than any other country. In this small area, a volcano erupts about every five years! There are about 200 volcanoes in Iceland. It is one of the most active volcano areas in the world. In 1963, a volcano created the island of Surtsey. In four years, this island grew to about one square mile and rose to more than 560 feet.

**Tip**
Don't try to memorize facts about Iceland. Read to understand the most important ideas. You can look back at the passage later to locate facts you need to know.

Much of Iceland is covered with the sparkling ice of glaciers. The third largest glacier in the world is located in Iceland. Only the glaciers in Antarctica and Greenland are bigger.

Although Iceland lies just below the Arctic Circle and is partly covered by glaciers, the country is warmer than you might expect. The waters of the Gulf Stream in the Atlantic Ocean warm Iceland's climate. The average July temperature is a very comfortable 51° Fahrenheit. Of course, in winter it gets much colder.

Only about 250,000 people live in Iceland. This number is less than half of the population of Memphis, Tennessee. Most people who live in Iceland live in Reykjavik, the capital city. Iceland attracts visitors who like open spaces, nature, and outdoor activities such as hiking.

**Tip**
You probably don't recognize the proper noun *Reykjavik*, but notice that the author explains it in the text.

Name ______________________________

**1 Iceland is called "A Land of Fire and Ice" because**

**A** it has the world's third-largest glacier
**B** it has both volcanoes and glaciers
**C** it is warmed by the Gulf Stream
**D** it has 200 volcanoes

> **Tip**
> Reread the beginning of the article, if necessary, to recall the author's explanation of what the title means.

**2 Based on information in the passage, you can conclude that a glacier is**

**A** a large mass of ice
**B** a kind of volcano
**C** an island
**D** a hot spring

**3 Which of the following statements is an opinion?**

**A** There are about 200 volcanoes in Iceland.
**B** Iceland is about the same size as Virginia.
**C** The July temperature of 51° Fahrenheit is very comfortable.
**D** The population of Iceland is about half the population of Memphis, Tennessee.

> **Tip**
> Remember that an opinion tells what someone thinks or feels about something. The statement cannot be proved.

**4 Who would probably enjoy visiting Iceland?**

**A** someone who likes peaceful places and unspoiled nature
**B** someone who likes warm weather and sandy beaches
**C** someone who enjoys visiting art museums and theaters
**D** someone who likes to shop and travel from city to city by train

**5 Write a sentence to summarize this article.**

______________________________

______________________________

______________________________

> **Tip**
> Think about what should and should not be included in a summary. Your sentence should tell only the most important idea or ideas.

| | | | | |
|---|---|---|---|---|
| 1 | Ⓐ | Ⓑ | Ⓒ | Ⓓ |
| 2 | Ⓐ | Ⓑ | Ⓒ | Ⓓ |
| 3 | Ⓐ | Ⓑ | Ⓒ | Ⓓ |
| 4 | Ⓐ | Ⓑ | Ⓒ | Ⓓ |





GO ON

Name ______________________________

# *Directions*

**Read this paragraph from a report a student wrote about a bird called the kiwi. It has several mistakes that need correcting. Then answer Questions 6 through 8.**

> **The Kiwi**
>
> [1] The furry, brown kiwi does not look much like a bird. [2] It has whiskers like a cat, and its feathers looks like a mouse's fur coat. [3] Rabbits and other animals also have whiskers. [4] The kiwi cannot fly. [5] It can walk almost silently on its soft feet. [6] It lives in the mountain forests of New Zealand.

**6 Which sentence does not belong in this paragraph?**

**A** Sentence 2

**B** Sentence 3

**C** Sentence 4

**D** Sentence 6

> **Tip**
> Think about the topic of the paragraph. The sentence that does not belong is the one that does not tell about that topic.

**7 How can the error in Sentence 2 be corrected?**

**A** by changing *has* to *have*

**B** by changing *its* to *it's*

**C** by changing *looks* to *look*

**D** by changing *mouse's* to *mouses'*

**8 Choose the best way to combine Sentences 4 and 5.**

**A** The kiwi cannot fly it can walk almost silently on its soft feet.

**B** The kiwi cannot fly, it can walk almost silently on its soft feet.

**C** The kiwi cannot fly and it can walk almost silently on its soft feet.

**D** The kiwi cannot fly, but it can walk almost silently on its soft feet.

> **Tip**
> Look carefully to see whether answer choices are run-on sentences or comma splices. Choose the compound sentence that is written and punctuated correctly.



| | |
|---|---|
| 6 | Ⓐ Ⓑ Ⓒ Ⓓ |
| 7 | Ⓐ Ⓑ Ⓒ Ⓓ |
| 8 | Ⓐ Ⓑ Ⓒ Ⓓ |

Name ______________________________

## *Directions*

**Look at the underlined part of the sentence. Choose the answer that shows the correct punctuation for that part. If the underlined part is correct, mark "Correct as is."**

**9 The mother duck swam away and the ducklings followed her.**

**A** away, and

**B** away. and

**C** away and,

**D** Correct as is

> **Tip**
> Identify the structure of the sentence to help you decide on the correct punctuation.

**10 Read the sentence. Choose the answer that shows which word in the sentence should be capitalized. If the capitalization is correct, mark "Correct as is."**

**The city of oslo is the capital of Norway.**

**A** city

**B** oslo

**C** capital

**D** Correct as is

**11 Choose the word that is spelled correctly and completes the sentence.**

**The loud thunder ______ the horses.**

**A** scared

**B** scaired

**C** scairred

**D** scard

> **Tip**
> Remember to use a comma and a conjunction to join the two parts of your sentence.

**12 Write a compound sentence about a place you would like to visit. Capitalize and punctuate correctly.**

______________________________

______________________________

______________________________

______________________________



| | |
|---|---|
| 9 | Ⓐ Ⓑ Ⓒ Ⓓ |
| 10 | Ⓐ Ⓑ Ⓒ Ⓓ |
| 11 | Ⓐ Ⓑ Ⓒ Ⓓ |

STOP

Name ____________________

*Directions*

**Read the poem below. Then answer Questions 1 through 5. You may look back at the poem.**

# Hot Enough for You?

The thermometer said seventy-two.
That's not too hot at all.
"Seventy-two?" my mother said.
"That's only in the hall."

"It's much hotter," my mother said,
"outside in the sun.
I was out there with the neighbors,
and it's melting everyone!"

> **Tip**
> Does the mother mean that the neighbors are actually melting, or is she exaggerating to make a point?

It must be very hot indeed
to make our neighbors melt!
Did they drip like candles made of wax?
I wonder how that felt.

How very hot does it have to be
to cause us to perspire,
and how much hotter yet
to make us feel like we're on fire?

Maybe it's ninety in the sun,
maybe a hundred and three.
I'm going out to play right now.
How hot can it be?

If I get too hot and start to melt,
I'll play beneath a tree,
but numbers on a thermometer
can't tell me how hot to be!

> **Tip**
> Think about why the narrator of the poem might decide to play beneath a tree if it gets too hot.

Name ______________________________

**1 Which picture shows the place mentioned in the poem where the temperature is seventy-two?**

A B C D

**2 What does the mother mean when she says that the neighbors are "melting"?**

**A** They have all gone inside.
**B** They are feeling very warm.
**C** They are burning candles.
**D** They are eating ice cream.

**3 The narrator compares the neighbors to**

**A** candles
**B** thermometers
**C** the sun
**D** trees

> **Tip**
> Look back at the poem to find the comparison. The word *like* is a clue that two things are being compared.

**4 Which of these is <u>not</u> an example of an effect caused by heat?**

**A** Candles melt and drip.
**B** People perspire.
**C** The thermometer rises.
**D** The sun shines.

> **Tip**
> Ask yourself whether each answer choice is something that happens as a result of the heat. Choose the one that is *not* caused by heat.

**5 Which of these is true about the way the poem is written?**

**A** The first and third lines always rhyme.
**B** The second and fourth lines always rhyme.
**C** The first two lines and the second two lines rhyme.
**D** Some lines rhyme, but there is no pattern.

> **Tip**
> To answer this question, look back at the poem to find the words that rhyme and identify the pattern.

| | |
|---|---|
| 1 | Ⓐ Ⓑ Ⓒ Ⓓ |
| 2 | Ⓐ Ⓑ Ⓒ Ⓓ |
| 3 | Ⓐ Ⓑ Ⓒ Ⓓ |
| 4 | Ⓐ Ⓑ Ⓒ Ⓓ |
| 5 | Ⓐ Ⓑ Ⓒ Ⓓ |



GO ON

Name ____________________

*Directions*

**Rick wrote a letter to his friend. For Questions 6 through 8, choose the answer with the correct capitalization and punctuation.**

(6) ________

(7) ________

The weather here has been very hot, but my friends and I find ways to have fun and stay cool. How is the weather where you live? What kinds of things have you been doing this summer?

(8) ________

**6** **A** May 19, 2003
**B** May 19 2003
**C** may 19, 2003
**D** may 19 2003

**7** **A** dear Matt,
**B** dear matt
**C** Dear Matt
**D** Dear Matt,

**8** **A** your Friend,
**B** your friend
**C** Your friend,
**D** Your Friend

**Tip**
When you choose the date, greeting, and closing for the letter, remember to check both the capitalization and the punctuation to be sure they are correct.



| | |
|---|---|
| **6** | Ⓐ Ⓑ Ⓒ Ⓓ |
| **7** | Ⓐ Ⓑ Ⓒ Ⓓ |
| **8** | Ⓐ Ⓑ Ⓒ Ⓓ |

Name ______________________________

## *Directions*

**Look at the underlined part of the sentence. Choose the answer that shows the correct punctuation for that part. If the underlined part is correct, mark "Correct as is."**

**9** **Because it rained, my bike got wet.**

**A** Because it rained

**B** Because, it rained

**C** Because it rained.

**D** Correct as is

> **Tip**
> Notice that the sentence begins with a dependent clause.

**10** **Choose the word that correctly completes the sentence.**

**Yesterday I _____ two new flowers in the garden.**

**A** see

**B** seen

**C** saw

**D** sees

> **Tip**
> The word *yesterday* is a clue that the sentence tells about an action in the past, so the past tense verb is the correct answer choice.

**11** **Read the phrases. Choose the phrase containing an underlined word that is spelled wrong. If all the underlined words are spelled correctly, mark "All correct."**

**A** all the children

**B** a serprise party

**C** birthday cake

**D** All correct

**12** **Write a sentence about something you like to do in the summer. Include a dependent clause in your sentence. Capitalize and punctuate correctly.**

______________________________

______________________________



| | |
|---|---|
| 9 | Ⓐ Ⓑ Ⓒ Ⓓ |
| 10 | Ⓐ Ⓑ Ⓒ Ⓓ |
| 11 | Ⓐ Ⓑ Ⓒ Ⓓ |

STOP

Name ______________________________

*Directions*

**Read the article below. Then answer Questions 1 through 5. You may look back at the article.**

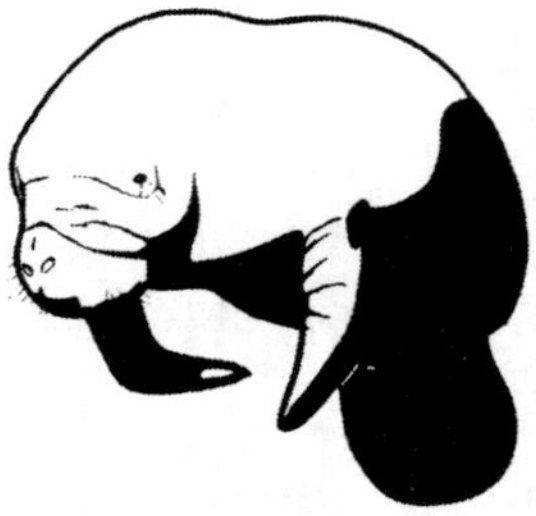

# Gentle Giants

Manatees are giant mammals that live in warm, shallow ocean waters. They are harmless animals that feed on huge amounts of sea grass, water lettuce, and other water plants. A full-grown manatee can eat 100 to 150 pounds of plants a day!

**Tip**
If you are not familiar with the animal described in this passage, don't let that confuse you. Read on to learn more about it.

Florida is home to the world's largest manatee population—about 2,400 manatees. The population grows slowly because female manatees usually give birth to only one infant every two to five years. The low birth rate is one reason why the manatee is in danger of disappearing forever.

Humans and their speedboats are the biggest problem for manatees. Manatees are slow swimmers that swim close to the water's surface. The propeller blades of a fast-moving motorboat can strike a manatee and cause serious injury.

There are ways to help keep manatees safe. Because fast-moving boats can't see the animals underwater until it is too late, experts support slow-speed zones for boaters in areas where manatees live. Another idea is to have boaters place propeller guards on their boats.

**Tip**
The first sentence in a paragraph is often the topic sentence. It states the main idea of the paragraph. As you read, use the topic sentence to focus your attention on important details in the other sentences.

One way to help manatees is to protect their homes by keeping waters clean and limiting building on nearby land. Protecting manatees in these ways may help to make sure these interesting and gentle creatures will be around for a long time.

| Manatee Facts | |
|---|---|
| weight at birth | 60–70 pounds |
| adult weight | 1,500–1,800 pounds |
| food per day | 100–150 pounds of plants |
| life span | 60 years |
| average swimming speed | 3–5 miles per hour |
| top swimming speed | 20 miles per hour |

**Tip**
Nonfiction texts sometimes include graphic aids, such as charts or maps, that show information not given in the text.





GO ON

Name ______________________________

1 **If humans don't take action to protect manatees,**

**A** the manatees' food supply could run out

**B** boaters will need propeller guards

**C** manatees could disappear

**D** manatees will leave Florida for new homes in other places

2 **You can find out the rate that manatees swim in miles per hour**

**A** by skimming the article

**B** by looking at the chart

**C** by rereading the text

**D** by using both the text and the chart

> **Tip**
> The text of the article mentions that manatees are slow swimmers, but does it give the swimming speed in miles per hour?

3 **What information about manatees is found in both the chart and the text?**

**A** the amount of food eaten per day

**B** the weight of a full-grown adult

**C** what foods manatees eat

**D** how many manatees there are in Florida

4 **You can tell from the article that the author**

**A** has a boat with a propeller guard

**B** thinks people should not own boats

**C** wants readers to visit Florida

**D** cares about manatees

> **Tip**
> When you first read the answer choices, you may find that more than one is possibly correct. Decide which one is most likely or possible, based on what you read in the article.

5 **Write a sentence to summarize this article.**

______________________________

______________________________

______________________________



| | |
|---|---|
| 1 | Ⓐ Ⓑ Ⓒ Ⓓ |
| 2 | Ⓐ Ⓑ Ⓒ Ⓓ |
| 3 | Ⓐ Ⓑ Ⓒ Ⓓ |
| 4 | Ⓐ Ⓑ Ⓒ Ⓓ |

GO ON

Name ______________________________

## Directions

**Choose the sentences that best develop the topic sentence.**

**6 Prairie dogs live in underground tunnels, or burrows, that connect to one another.**

**A** A prairie is a large area of grassy land. Years ago, America's prairie lands were home to huge herds of bison, or buffaloes.

**B** People build tunnels to run roads and railroads through mountains. Tunnels also allow people to travel beneath bodies of water.

**C** Pet dogs owned by people often like to dig holes in the ground. This can be very annoying to homeowners.

**D** These burrows can spread out for acres. Inside their burrows, the prairie dogs live in family groups.

> **Tip**
> All of the choices include words used in the topic sentence. The correct choice is the one that gives more information about the main idea expressed in the topic sentence.

**7 What is the best pattern to use for organizing a passage that begins with this topic sentence?**

**A** cause and effect

**B** compare and contrast

**C** main idea and details

**D** sequence

> **Tip**
> Reread the topic sentence and the sentences you chose as your answer for Question 6. What pattern or text structure do you recognize?

**8 For what purpose would this passage be written?**

**A** to entertain

**B** to inform

**C** to describe

**D** to persuade



6 Ⓐ Ⓑ Ⓒ Ⓓ
7 Ⓐ Ⓑ Ⓒ Ⓓ
8 Ⓐ Ⓑ Ⓒ Ⓓ

Name ______________________________

## *Directions*

**Look at the underlined part of the sentence. Choose the answer that shows the correct punctuation for that part. If the underlined part is correct, mark "Correct as is."**

**9 Scientists tell us that animals are sometimes harmed, when new structures are built.**

**A** harmed when

**B** harmed when,

**C** harmed," when

**D** Correct as is

> **Tip**
> The word *when* in this sentence introduces a dependent clause. Think about where in the sentence the dependent clause is located. Does this part of the sentence need any form of punctuation?

**10 Read the sentence. Then choose the answer in which the word *look* has the same meaning as it does in the sentence.**

**Kate went to school with a happy look on her face.**

**A** look at a picture

**B** take a look

**C** pears look ripe

**D** a look of embarrassment

> **Tip**
> Notice that *look* is used as a noun in the sentence. Find the phrases in which *look* is used as a noun. Then decide which has the same meaning.

**11 Choose the word that is spelled correctly and completes the sentence.**

**The crowd laughed when the whale ______.**

**A** spowted

**B** spouted

**C** spoughted

**D** spooted

**12 Write a complex sentence that tells how people can help endangered wildlife. Capitalize and punctuate correctly.**

______________________________

______________________________

| | |
|---|---|
| 9 | Ⓐ Ⓑ Ⓒ Ⓓ |
| 10 | Ⓐ Ⓑ Ⓒ Ⓓ |
| 11 | Ⓐ Ⓑ Ⓒ Ⓓ |

STOP

Name ______________________________

## *Directions*

**WRITE AN INFORMATIVE COMPOSITION** **Think of important information about the environment that you have learned in school or from another source. Write a composition to inform others about these facts and ideas. Organize your composition according to main idea and details. Include details that support your main idea.**

**Use the organizer below to plan your composition, and write it on a separate sheet of paper. When you are finished with the draft, use the Writer's Checklist to revise and edit your work. Then make a final copy of your composition.**

**Main Idea:**

| **Supporting Details** | **Supporting Details** |
|---|---|
| ______________ | ______________ |
| ______________ | ______________ |
| ______________ | ______________ |

Name ______________________________

### *Writer's Checklist*

- ❏ Do you introduce your topic in a clear and interesting way?
- ❏ Do you state your main idea in a topic sentence?
- ❏ Do you present details that explain and support your main idea?
- ❏ Did you arrange your details in a logical order?
- ❏ Did you organize your composition in paragraphs?
- ❏ Did you include different types of sentences?
- ❏ Do you have any run-on sentences or fragments?
- ❏ Did you begin sentences and names of people with capital letters?
- ❏ Did you end sentences with the correct end marks?
- ❏ Did you try to spell each word correctly?

Name ______________________________

*Directions*

**Read the story below. Then answer Questions 1 through 5. You may look back at the story.**

# Only One Choice

> **Tip**
> The title often gives a clue about important events in a story. Read this story to find out what choice a character has to make and what he or she decides to do.

Ben had dreamed all his life about doing something exciting. Aunt Molly told Ben about her experience teaching river rafting. She described how it felt to ride the currents and coast the rapids. Then she asked Ben to go rafting with her. Finally, he had a chance to make his dream come true!

On the big day, Aunt Molly was to pick up Ben at 10 A.M. As Ben filled his backpack, he heard Mom yell, "Ben! Ben! Hurry!" He raced downstairs and saw his little sister, Tori, lying on the kitchen floor.

"I fell," Tori said. "My leg hurts, and my head feels funny."

"Call an ambulance, Ben," said Mom. "I'll sit with Tori."

Ben dialed 911. It was 9:15. Worried about Tori, he hoped the ambulance would come right away. It arrived at 9:20, and two workers gently carried Tori and placed her inside the vehicle.

"She hit her head," Mom told them.

"She'll probably be all right, but we should check it out completely," said the driver. "You can climb in the back with her, folks."

Ben was about to jump in the ambulance when Mom reminded him to stay behind so he wouldn't miss his rafting trip. With all the excitement, he had forgotten about the trip! Ben looked at his sister and saw tears in her eyes.

> **Tip**
> As you read, make predictions about what might happen next in the story. What choice do you think Ben will make?

"I want Ben to go with me," Tori whispered to Mom.

Ben thought for a second. Then he said, "An ambulance ride will be enough excitement for me today!"

Name ______________________________

**1 Which picture shows an event that did not result from Tori's fall?**

A

B

C

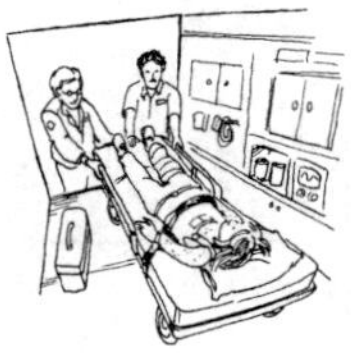
D

> **Tip**
> Tori's fall was the cause of the events shown in three of the pictures. The correct choice shows the event that was *not* caused by the fall.

**2 The problem Ben faces in this story is**

**A** figuring out how to get help for his sister
**B** deciding whether to go with Tori or to go on his trip
**C** getting his mother to let him go on the rafting trip
**D** being afraid that he will get hurt if he tries river rafting

**3 You can draw the conclusion that the title "Only One Choice" means**

**A** there is only one choice Ben can make and feel good about
**B** Ben has only one choice because his mother tells him what to do
**C** Ben's mother makes the right choice about calling an ambulance
**D** Ben makes the wrong choice about riding in the ambulance

> **Tip**
> To draw a conclusion about the title, use details from the story and your own knowledge to figure out what the title means.

**4 The words that best describe Ben are**

**A** selfish and uncaring
**B** honest and brave
**C** friendly and talkative
**D** caring and unselfish

**5 What do you think might happen next in this story?**

**A** Ben will blame Tori for making him miss the rafting trip.
**B** Ben will decide he is afraid to go rafting.
**C** Aunt Molly and Ben will plan another rafting trip.
**D** Ben will lose interest in rafting and not think about it again.

> **Tip**
> Rereading the first paragraph to recall how Ben feels about rafting may help you eliminate some answer choices.

| | |
|---|---|
| 1 | Ⓐ Ⓑ Ⓒ Ⓓ |
| 2 | Ⓐ Ⓑ Ⓒ Ⓓ |
| 3 | Ⓐ Ⓑ Ⓒ Ⓓ |
| 4 | Ⓐ Ⓑ Ⓒ Ⓓ |
| 5 | Ⓐ Ⓑ Ⓒ Ⓓ |

Name ______________________________

# *Directions*

**Look at this table of contents from a book called *Get Ready for Rafting!* Then answer Questions 6 through 8.**

**Contents**



**6 Which chapter would you look at to find out what kind of shoes or footgear you would need for a rafting trip?**

**A** Chapter 1

**B** Chapter 2

**C** Chapter 3

**D** Chapter 4

> **Tip**
> Read the chapter titles. Think about the kind of information you might find in each chapter. Which chapter might tell about shoes or footgear?

**7 Which chapter has an exclamatory sentence for a title?**

**A** Chapter 2

**B** Chapter 3

**C** Chapter 4

**D** Chapter 5

**8 A student is reading Chapter 4. Which of these topics is probably covered in that chapter?**

**A** the best rivers for rafting trips

**B** what clothes to pack for a rafting trip

**C** how to tell if a rafting guide is well-qualified

**D** how to avoid accidents and injuries

> **Tip**
> Find the title of Chapter 4 in the table of contents. Pick the answer choice that is most likely to be covered in that chapter.



| | |
|---|---|
| 6 | Ⓐ Ⓑ Ⓒ Ⓓ |
| 7 | Ⓐ Ⓑ Ⓒ Ⓓ |
| 8 | Ⓐ Ⓑ Ⓒ Ⓓ |

Name ______________________________

*Directions*

**Read the sentence. Choose the answer that shows which words in the sentence should be capitalized. If the capitalization is correct, mark "Correct as is."**

**9 The coryville ambulance Corps is raising money to buy a new vehicle.**

**A** The coryville ambulance corps is raising money to buy a new vehicle.

**B** The Coryville ambulance Corps is raising money to buy a new vehicle.

**C** The Coryville Ambulance Corps is raising money to buy a new vehicle.

**D** Correct as is

**Tip**
Remember that each important word of a proper noun begins with a capital letter.

**10 Choose the word that correctly completes the sentence.**

**The girl said the backpack was ______.**

**A** hers

**B** her's

**C** she

**D** she's

**11 Read the phrases. Choose the phrase containing an underlined word that is spelled wrong. If all the underlined words are spelled correctly, mark "All correct."**

**A** silver and gold

**B** bells jingle

**C** in my pocket

**D** All correct

**12 Write a sentence that tells about a person or place you care about. Use at least one proper noun in the sentence. Capitalize and punctuate correctly.**

______________________________

______________________________

______________________________

**Tip**
Be sure to use a proper noun, a noun that names a particular person or place, in your sentence.

| | |
|---|---|
| 9 | Ⓐ Ⓑ Ⓒ Ⓓ |
| 10 | Ⓐ Ⓑ Ⓒ Ⓓ |
| 11 | Ⓐ Ⓑ Ⓒ Ⓓ |

STOP

Name ____________________

*D*irections

**Read the story below. Then answer Questions 1 through 5. You may look back at the story.**

# Changing Chores

"I'm tired of vacuuming," Teri said.

"Well, it's better than taking out the garbage," her brother Tom said. He picked up the heavy, smelly bag and carried it outside. Teri watched him. Taking the garbage out was not fun, but she was sure it had to be better than vacuuming. She hated the high-pitched squeal, and she hated hauling around that monster of a machine.

"I have an idea," Teri said when Tom returned. "Why don't we switch jobs? Just for a week."

"Good idea," he answered.

By the end of the week, Teri decided that Tom was right. Garbage duty was terrible. The garbage cans always smelled. Also, the garbage had to be taken out every day! Vacuuming was just a once-a-week chore. "Let's switch back," Teri suggested.

At first, Tom didn't say anything. Finally, he said, "I like vacuuming. I pretend that I'm searching for treasure. I even like the sound the vacuum cleaner makes. It's a lot more fun than taking out the garbage. Couldn't we switch for good?"

Teri thought about it. Did she really hate garbage duty that much? At least she was able to go outside, and the job didn't take very long. It wasn't fun, but maybe it was better than vacuuming. Besides, it would make Tom happy, and he was a pretty good brother.

"All right," Teri said, with a laugh. "Tom the Treasure Hunter, you've got yourself a deal!"

**Tip**
When a story has dialogue in quotation marks, pay careful attention to be sure you know which character is speaking each time.

**Tip**
The details in this paragraph explain Teri's thoughts about garbage duty. Keep reading to find out what Tom thinks of vacuuming.

**Tip**
You don't need to remember all the reasons Teri has for agreeing to the switch. You can reread them later if you need to answer questions about them.

Name ______________________________

1 **Why does Teri call the vacuum cleaner a *monster of a machine*?**

A The noise bothers her.

B It is very large and very heavy.

C It is unpleasant to use.

D It is actually a monster robot disguised as a vacuum cleaner.

**Tip**
If you don't recall what Teri means, scan the story to find the phrase *monster of a machine.* Then reread the sentence to figure out why Teri compares the machine to a monster.

2 **How does Teri compare garbage duty and vacuuming?**

A Both have to be done every day.

B Both smell bad.

C Both are noisy.

D Both are unpleasant jobs.

3 **Which of these is <u>not</u> a reason why Teri agrees to switch jobs in the end?**

A She likes going outside.

B She thinks garbage duty is fun.

C Garbage duty doesn't take long.

D She likes doing something nice for Tom.

**Tip**
Pay attention to the word *not* in the question. If necessary, reread the last part of the story to recall Teri's reasons for agreeing.

4 **Here are some events from the story. Place the events in order from 1 to 4 by writing the numbers in the boxes next to each sentence.**

☐ Teri decides she doesn't like garbage duty.

☐ Teri watches Tom take the garbage out.

☐ Teri tells Tom her idea to switch jobs.

☐ Tom tells Teri that he likes vacuuming.

5 **Which statement might be the theme, or lesson, of this story?**

A Two heads are better than one.

B The best job is the one you enjoy.

C Nobody should work all the time.

D Work goes faster when you work together.

**Tip**
The theme of a story is like the lesson of a folktale. Think about what the characters did and what they learned at the end of the story. What did Teri learn?

| | |
|---|---|
| 1 | Ⓐ Ⓑ Ⓒ Ⓓ |
| 2 | Ⓐ Ⓑ Ⓒ Ⓓ |
| 3 | Ⓐ Ⓑ Ⓒ Ⓓ |
| 5 | Ⓐ Ⓑ Ⓒ Ⓓ |





GO ON

Name ______________________________________________

## *Directions*

**Read this paragraph from a report a student wrote about electricity. It has several mistakes that need correcting. Then answer Questions 6 through 8.**

> **Electricity**
>
> [1] Electricity is the form of energy we use for light and often for heating and cooling. [2] Many of our most biggest machines and smallest appliances run on electricity. [3] Without electricity it would be difficult to live as comfortably as we do.

**6 Which of these sentences would be the best topic sentence for the paragraph?**

**A** Some homes are heated by oil or gas.

**B** Human beings get energy from the food we eat.

**C** We can save energy by turning off lights when we leave a room.

**D** We use many different kinds of energy, but electricity is the one we use most.

> **Tip**
> Try rereading the paragraph with each of the choices as the first sentence. Which sentence states the main idea that the rest of the sentences support?

**7 What is the best way to rewrite Sentence 2?**

**A** Many of our most big machines and most small appliances run on electricity.

**B** Many of our more big machines and smallest appliances run on electricity.

**C** Many of our biggest machines and smallest appliances run on electricity.

**D** Many of our most biggest machines and most smallest appliances run on electricity.

**8 Which word in Sentence 3 should be followed by a comma?**

**A** electricity

**B** it

**C** would

**D** comfortably

> **Tip**
> If you are not sure where the comma belongs, try eliminating incorrect answers. For example, commas are not used to separate subjects and verbs, or helping verbs and main verbs.

| | | | | |
|---|---|---|---|---|
| 6 | Ⓐ | Ⓑ | Ⓒ | Ⓓ |
| 7 | Ⓐ | Ⓑ | Ⓒ | Ⓓ |
| 8 | Ⓐ | Ⓑ | Ⓒ | Ⓓ |

Name ______________________________

## *Directions*

**Look at the underlined part of the sentence. Choose the answer that shows the correct punctuation for that part. If the underlined part is correct, mark "Correct as is."**

**9 Mr. Arnold said, "Good morning, class."**

A said Good

B said "Good

C said, Good

D Correct as is

> **Tip**
> Notice that the sentence is quoting someone's exact words. How does an author punctuate the characters' dialogue in a story?

**10 Choose the word that correctly completes the sentence.**

**______ all the children finished their work?**

A Have

B Has

C Do

D Does

**11 Read the phrases. Choose the phrase containing an underlined word that is spelled wrong. If all the underlined words are spelled correctly, mark "All correct."**

A a worried frown

B as darkness fell

C a cheerfull tune

D All correct

> **Tip**
> To figure out the correct spelling of a word with a suffix added, it is helpful to know the correct spelling of common suffixes such as *-ful, -ness,* and *-ed.*

**12 Write a sentence about chores that children can do to help around the house. Use at least one plural noun in the sentence. Capitalize and punctuate correctly.**

______________________________

______________________________



| | |
|---|---|
| 9 | Ⓐ Ⓑ Ⓒ Ⓓ |
| 10 | Ⓐ Ⓑ Ⓒ Ⓓ |
| 11 | Ⓐ Ⓑ Ⓒ Ⓓ |

STOP

Name ______________________________

*Directions*

**Read the story below. Then answer Questions 1 through 5. You may look back at the story.**

# Queen of the House

Violet was the queen of the house. Visitors could spot her black and gray stripes curled up on the leather couch, under the blue chair, in the middle of the bed, or anywhere else she chose to sleep at any time of day. When anyone reached down to stroke the soft fur between her ears, she would purr contentedly.

> **Tip**
> If you do not recognize a long word, use familiar word parts and the context to figure out its meaning.

The only thing that could disturb Violet's peace of mind was a visit from Melrose, who lived next door. Melrose was a big orange cat. He always ate Violet's food, as well as his own. He even sat on her favorite sunny windowsill to watch birds.

Violet's owner, Barbara, was always baby-sitting this younger cat for some reason. No reason, however, was good enough for Violet.

> **Tip**
> Notice that a new character, Barbara, is introduced in this paragraph. Unlike the other characters, Barbara is a person, not a cat.

One day, Violet decided she had had enough of Melrose. When Barbara woke up that morning, she found Melrose in his usual place on the windowsill. Violet was nowhere to be found. Barbara remembered hearing angry hisses from Violet when she fed the cats the night before. Had the noises been a signal? Barbara looked all through the house, in every cabinet and closet, and under every bed and chair.

Two days later, Barbara still had not found Violet. Melrose's owner came by to take Melrose home and to thank Barbara for taking care of him. Barbara had just gone back in her house and closed the door when she heard a familiar sound. It was Violet meowing at the door! Barbara opened the door and scooped up Violet, who purred loudly. She was happy to be home again and to be the queen of her own house once more.

> **Tip**
> Use clues from the story to help you draw conclusions about where Violet was and why she was missing.

Name ______________________________

**1 Violet is called the *queen of the house* because**

**A** she is fussy about her food

**B** she gets her own way

**C** she does not like Melrose

**D** she lives in a castle

> **Tip**
> Use clues from the story and what you know about queens to help you pick the best answer.

**2 Melrose's visits disturb Violet because**

**A** Barbara pays more attention to Melrose than to Violet

**B** Melrose makes angry hissing noises

**C** Melrose eats her food and sits on her windowsill

**D** she doesn't like Melrose's owner

**3 Which picture <u>best</u> shows the meaning of the word contentedly?**

**A**

**B**

**C**

**D**

**4 What conclusion can you draw about why Violet disappears?**

**A** She decides to live at Melrose's house.

**B** She gets lost and can't find her way home.

**C** She wants to show Barbara how she feels.

**D** She is looking for a new owner.

> **Tip**
> Authors do not always tell everything about a character. Use clues from the story and your own knowledge to draw a conclusion.

**5 This story can best be described as**

**A** historical fiction

**B** a biography

**C** a folktale

**D** realistic fiction

| | |
|---|---|
| 1 | Ⓐ Ⓑ Ⓒ Ⓓ |
| 2 | Ⓐ Ⓑ Ⓒ Ⓓ |
| 3 | Ⓐ Ⓑ Ⓒ Ⓓ |
| 4 | Ⓐ Ⓑ Ⓒ Ⓓ |
| 5 | Ⓐ Ⓑ Ⓒ Ⓓ |



GO ON

Name ______________________________

## *Directions*

**Read this poster that a student made. Then answer Questions 6 through 8.**

**CAT RESCUE CAR WASH**

Saturday and Sunday

**May 22–23, 10 A.M. to 4 P.M.**

8935 Hancock Road

Cars: $3.00 Vans and Trucks: $4.00

All money goes to support the work of Cat Rescue. We need your support!

**6 What is the main purpose of this poster?**

**A** to tell what Cat Rescue does

**B** to tell where cats can be adopted

**C** to inform people that the car wash costs more for trucks and vans than for cars

**D** to persuade people to go to the car wash

> **Tip**
> Read all of the answer choices before you decide. The poster gives certain information, but giving that information may not be the *main* purpose of the poster.

**7 The poster tells people that**

**A** all money goes to support Cat Rescue

**B** getting a car washed will cost $4.00

**C** the car wash is on Monday

**D** the car wash begins at noon

**8 The poster probably has pictures of cats because**

**A** cats are cute

**B** they will get people's attention

**C** they will make people want to get a cat

**D** cats will be given away at the car wash

> **Tip**
> To answer this question, think about the purpose of a poster or a sign.



6 Ⓐ Ⓑ Ⓒ Ⓓ
7 Ⓐ Ⓑ Ⓒ Ⓓ
8 Ⓐ Ⓑ Ⓒ Ⓓ

Name ______________________________

## *Directions*

**Read the phrases. Look for an underlined word that contains a usage error. If the underlined words are used correctly, mark "All correct."**

**9** **A** <u>mail</u> a letter
**B** <u>road</u> a bike
**C** <u>right</u> turn
**D** All correct

> **Tip**
> The underlined words are all homophones. Think about whether each is spelled correctly or whether another word that sounds the same but is spelled differently should be used instead.

**10 Which sentence is written correctly?**

**A** The sisters saw three blue eggs in a robins nest in their friends yard.
**B** The sister's saw three blue egg's in a robin's nest in their friend's yard.
**C** The sisters saw three blue egg's in a robins nest in their friend's yard.
**D** The sisters saw three blue eggs in a robin's nest in their friend's yard.

**11 Read the phrases. Choose the phrase containing an underlined word that is spelled wrong. If all the underlined words are spelled correctly, mark "All correct."**

**A** <u>nod</u> your head
**B** hands and <u>nees</u>
**C** giraffe's long <u>neck</u>
**D** All correct

> **Tip**
> Watch out for words with silent letters, such as *know* and *knife.*

**12 Write a sentence about pets. Use at least one possessive noun in the sentence. Capitalize and punctuate correctly.**

______________________________

______________________________

______________________________

| | |
|---|---|
| 9 | Ⓐ Ⓑ Ⓒ Ⓓ |
| 10 | Ⓐ Ⓑ Ⓒ Ⓓ |
| 11 | Ⓐ Ⓑ Ⓒ Ⓓ |

STOP

Name ______________________________

## *Directions*

**Read the poem below. Then answer Questions 1 through 5. You may look back at the poem.**

# Hot and Cold

Have you ever been to the desert?
It's a land of heat and sand.
The sun shines hot in the sky.
The air is blazing and dry.
You're baked like a pie.
You might see a cactus nearby.
It's a land of heat and sand.

**Tip**
Notice that the title of the poem contains words that are opposites. Read the poem to find out what the title means.

Have you ever been to the Arctic?
It's a cold and icy land.
Everywhere you see snow,
Above, around, and below.
You feel frozen from head to toe.
You shiver as frigid winds blow.
It's a cold and icy land.

**Tip**
As you read the second verse of the poem, think about how the description of the Arctic differs from the description of the desert in the first verse.





GO ON

Name ____________________

**1 Which pair of words from the poem are antonyms?**

**A** cold, ice

**B** sand, snow

**C** blazing, frigid

**D** hot, dry

> **Tip**
> Remember that antonyms are words that have opposite meanings.

**2 The poem compares a person in the desert to**

**A** the sun

**B** sand

**C** a cactus

**D** a pie

> **Tip**
> Reread the verse of the poem that tells about the desert. Look for words such as *like* or *as* that signal a comparison.

**3 Which of these is true about the way the poem is written?**

**A** All the lines rhyme.

**B** None of the lines rhyme.

**C** The second and last lines of each verse are the same.

**D** Both verses have the same first and second lines.

**4 Which statement is true about this poem?**

**A** It tells how two different places are alike.

**B** It contrasts the desert and the Arctic.

**C** It tells why the Arctic is better than the desert.

**D** Its purpose is to persuade people to visit faraway places.

**5 Write two adjectives from the poem that describe the desert and two that describe the Arctic.**

> **Tip**
> Look back at the poem to find adjectives, words that describe nouns or pronouns.

| desert | Arctic |
|---|---|
| ____________________ | ____________________ |
| ____________________ | ____________________ |



| | |
|---|---|
| 1 | Ⓐ Ⓑ Ⓒ Ⓓ |
| 2 | Ⓐ Ⓑ Ⓒ Ⓓ |
| 3 | Ⓐ Ⓑ Ⓒ Ⓓ |
| 4 | Ⓐ Ⓑ Ⓒ Ⓓ |

GO ON

Name ________________________________

*Directions*

**Read this paragraph from a composition that a student wrote. Then answer Questions 6 through 8.**

**The Arctic and Antarctica**

[1] Would you want to live in either the Arctic or Antarctica? [2] It wouldn't be easy. [3] For one thing, it is difficult to adjust to the extremes of light and darkness. [4] The sun shines all night in the summer. [5] The sun doesn't come up at all in the winter.

**6 Which sentence would be the best closing sentence for the paragraph?**

**A** Polar bears have white fur that helps them blend in with the snowy background.

**B** Besides being dark, winter at both poles is extremely cold and windy.

**C** Scientists who study the polar regions need the right equipment.

**D** How would you like to live near the equator?

**Tip**
If you are not sure about an answer choice, reread the paragraph to see whether the sentence adds more information about the main idea.

**7 Choose the best way to combine Sentences 4 and 5.**

**A** The sun shines all night in the summer and doesn't come up at all in the winter.

**B** The sun shines all night in the summer, the sun doesn't come up at all in the winter.

**C** The sun shines all night in the summer it doesn't come up at all in the winter.

**D** The sun shines all night in the summer, or it doesn't come up at all in the winter.

**8 Which of these would be the best resource for finding maps of the Arctic region and Antarctica?**

**A** a dictionary

**B** a thesaurus

**C** an almanac

**D** an atlas

**Tip**
Read the question carefully. Notice that it asks specifically about maps. Which resource is a book of maps?

6 Ⓐ Ⓑ Ⓒ Ⓓ
7 Ⓐ Ⓑ Ⓒ Ⓓ
8 Ⓐ Ⓑ Ⓒ Ⓓ

Name ____________________

*Directions*

**Look at the underlined part of the sentence. Choose the answer that shows the correct capitalization and punctuation for that part. If the underlined part is correct, mark "Correct as is."**

**9** **Carla bought 1 lb of apples at the market.**

**A** 1 Lb
**B** 1 Lb.
**C** 1 lb.
**D** Correct as is

**10** **Choose the word or words that correctly complete the sentence.**

**Both _____ caps blew right off their heads.**

**A** boys
**B** boy's
**C** boys'
**D** boys's

**Tip**
You know from other words in the sentence that it tells about caps that belong to more than one boy. Choose the plural possessive form of the noun.

**11** **Choose the word that is spelled correctly and completes the sentence.**

**The high ______ peak was covered with snow.**

**A** mountain
**B** mountan
**C** mountin
**D** mounten

**12** **Write your return address and today's date, as you would in a business letter. Use at least one abbreviation. Capitalize and punctuate correctly.**

______________________________

______________________________

______________________________

**Tip**
Remember that periods are used after *most* abbreviations. Postal abbreviations for the 50 states are written with two capital letters and no period.



| | |
|---|---|
| 9 | Ⓐ Ⓑ Ⓒ Ⓓ |
| 10 | Ⓐ Ⓑ Ⓒ Ⓓ |
| 11 | Ⓐ Ⓑ Ⓒ Ⓓ |

STOP

Name ______________________________

*Directions*

**Read the article below. Then answer Questions 1 through 5. You may look back at the article.**

# Hello, Baby Blue

Sapphire is just a newborn baby, but she is much bigger than human babies. Sapphire is 23 feet long and weighs about 2 tons! Her mother thinks Sapphire is just the right size, and you would think so, too, if you were a blue whale.

> **Tip**
> The author does not tell you right away who or what Sapphire is. Read on to find out this information.

Like humans, whales are mammals and need air to breathe. Sapphire's mother pushed her to the surface of the water as soon as she was born so Sapphire could take her first breath of air.

Sapphire will stay close to her mother for the first year of her life, gaining as much as 200 pounds a day! She will also grow blubber, a thick layer of fat that helps keep whales warm in the cold ocean and provides them with food and energy. By the time Sapphire is finished growing, she may be as much as 95 feet long. Blue whales are the largest creatures of any kind ever to have lived on this planet.

> **Tip**
> Trying to remember all the numbers and other details in the article may confuse you. Read to understand the main idea. You can look back later to recall the details.

For now, Sapphire's food is her mother's milk. As she gets older, she will eat huge amounts of fish and small sea creatures called krill. Krill range in length from less than $\frac{1}{2}$ inch to less than 3 inches. Sapphire's mother can eat more than 4,000 pounds of krill in one feeding.

Blue whales make loud moaning sounds that can be heard underwater more than 100 miles away. Scientists believe that whales use these sounds to keep in touch with each other as they swim beneath the surface of the world's oceans.

Sapphire will soon be big enough to join the other whales in her group in their yearly swim from the warm waters of the tropics to the cold waters of the Arctic and Antarctica. Blue whales like Sapphire travel long distances and are found in every ocean of the world.

Name ______________________________

1 **You can tell that this article is an informational narrative because it**

**A** gives information about a topic

**B** tells about events that could be real

**C** is a story that presents information

**D** has animal characters

> **Tip**
> Read all the choices before you mark your answer. Choice A may seem like a good answer at first, but you may find a better one.

2 **Sapphire is different from human babies because**

**A** human babies breathe air

**B** Sapphire is much larger

**C** Sapphire is a mammal

**D** human babies require care

> **Tip**
> Try using each answer choice to complete the sentence. Keep in mind the key words *different from*. Which answer tells a way that Sapphire and human babies are different?

3 **The article explains that krill are**

**A** baby blue whales

**B** fish

**C** the sounds that blue whales make

**D** small sea creatures

> **Tip**
> If you don't remember the answer to this question, scan the article for the word *krill*. Then reread that part of the article.

4 **You can use information from the article to draw the conclusion that blue whales**

**A** prefer to be alone

**B** don't like other kinds of whales

**C** travel in groups

**D** spend most of their lives in one place

5 **Write a brief summary of the article.**

______________________________

______________________________

______________________________



1 Ⓐ Ⓑ Ⓒ Ⓓ
2 Ⓐ Ⓑ Ⓒ Ⓓ
3 Ⓐ Ⓑ Ⓒ Ⓓ
4 Ⓐ Ⓑ Ⓒ Ⓓ

GO ON

Name ______________________________

## *Directions*

**Read this paragraph from a story that a student wrote. It has several mistakes that need correcting. Then answer Questions 6 through 8.**

> **Keri's new pet**
>
> 1 Keri had always wanted a pet, but there was not enough room for a dog or cat in her family's small apartment. 2 One day, though, her dad come home with a surprise–a golden hamster.
>
> 3 He told Keri that the golden hamster is easy to keep as a pet it is gentle and can live in a small space. 4 Keri would need to give her new pet food, water, a place to exercise, and clean bedding.

**6 Choose the correct way to write the title. If the title is written correctly, mark "Correct as is."**

**A** Keri's New pet

**B** Keri's new Pet

**C** Keri's New Pet

**D** Correct as is

**7 Which sentence contains two complete thoughts and should be written as two sentences?**

**A** Sentence 1

**B** Sentence 2

**C** Sentence 3

**D** Sentence 4

> **Tip**
> Look for a run-on sentence made up of two independent clauses that are joined with no conjunction or punctuation between them.

**8 Which is the best way to rewrite Sentence 2?**

**A** One day, though, her dad comes home with a surprise—a golden hamster.

**B** One day, though, her dad came home with a surprise—a golden hamster.

**C** One day, though, her dad is coming home with a surprise—a golden hamster.

**D** One day, though, her dad has come home with a surprise—a golden hamster.

> **Tip**
> Check to be sure that the sentence you choose has the correct form of the verb and also the correct tense of the verb.

| | |
|---|---|
| 6 | Ⓐ Ⓑ Ⓒ Ⓓ |
| 7 | Ⓐ Ⓑ Ⓒ Ⓓ |
| 8 | Ⓐ Ⓑ Ⓒ Ⓓ |

Name ______________________________

*Directions*

**Look at the underlined part of the sentence. Choose the answer that shows the correct capitalization for that part. If the underlined part is correct, mark "Correct as is."**

**9 Jason went to Camp Wilson for two weeks.**

**A** camp wilson

**B** Camp wilson

**C** camp Wilson

**D** Correct as is

**10 What is the antecedent of the underlined word in the sentence below?**

**The boys were surprised because the turtles they found had red spots on their shells.**

**A** boys

**B** turtles

**C** spots

**D** shells

> **Tip**
> The antecedent of a pronoun is the noun or nouns to which the pronoun refers.

**11 Read the phrases. Choose the phrase containing an underlined word that is spelled wrong. If all the underlined words are spelled correctly, mark "All correct."**

**A** a brief glance

**B** gave a speach

**C** a greedy person

**D** All correct

> **Tip**
> All three underlined words have the long *e* sound, which can be spelled in different ways. Which word doesn't look right?

**12 Write a sentence about a favorite kind of animal. Use at least one pronoun. Circle each pronoun and the antecedent of each pronoun, and draw an arrow above the sentence from the pronoun to its antecedent. Capitalize and punctuate correctly.**

______________________________

______________________________

______________________________

| | |
|---|---|
| 9 | Ⓐ Ⓑ Ⓒ Ⓓ |
| 10 | Ⓐ Ⓑ Ⓒ Ⓓ |
| 11 | Ⓐ Ⓑ Ⓒ Ⓓ |

STOP

Name ______________________________

# *Directions*

**WRITE A PERSUASIVE COMPOSITION** Think of a change that students in your school could make that would make the school day more pleasant for everyone. Write a composition to persuade your fellow students to make this change. Include reasons and details to support your opinion.

Use the organizer below to plan your composition, and write it on a separate sheet of paper. When you are finished with the draft, use the Writer's Checklist to revise and edit your work. Then make a final copy of your composition.

**Opinion:**

**Reasons and Details**

Name ___

### *Writer's Checklist*

- ❑ Do you state your opinion in the opening sentence?
- ❑ Do you introduce your opinion in a way that captures your reader's attention?
- ❑ Do you present your reasons and details in a logical order?
- ❑ Do you conclude by restating your opinion and calling for action?
- ❑ Did you organize your composition in paragraphs?
- ❑ Did you include different types of sentences?
- ❑ Do you have any run-on sentences or fragments?
- ❑ Did you use correct grammar and punctuation?
- ❑ Did you begin sentences and proper nouns with capital letters?
- ❑ Did you try to spell each word correctly?



STOP

Name ________________________________

*Directions*

**Read the directions below. Then answer Questions 1 through 5. You may look back at the directions.**

# How to Make a Model Volcano

*Materials:*

stiff cardboard
glue
newspaper
flour and water paste
small plastic cup
baking soda
vinegar

**Tip**
A set of instructions often starts with a list of materials. Read the list carefully before you read the steps.

*Steps:*

1. On the cardboard, make a circle of glue 6 inches wide. Crumple newspaper into small balls. Place the balls onto the glue and build a cone shape about 6 inches tall.

2. Tear more newspaper into strips. Dip the strips into the flour and water paste. Then place them over the cone. Cover the cone with several layers of wet newspaper strips.

3. With your finger, poke a large hole, about 2 inches deep, at the top of the mountain. Put a small plastic cup into the opening. Let the mountain dry for several days.

4. Now you are ready to make the volcano erupt. Put 1 teaspoon of baking soda in the cup at the top of the volcano. Slowly pour 1 teaspoon of vinegar into the cup. Watch what happens!

**Tip**
Steps 1–3 tell how to construct your model volcano. Now read Step 4 to learn how to make the model volcano erupt.

Name ______________________________

**1 This passage is mostly about**

**A** how volcanoes erupt

**B** how to make a cone shape from newspapers

**C** the materials you need to make a model volcano

**D** how to make a model volcano that erupts

> **Tip**
> Read all the answer choices. Some of them include details from this set of directions, but only one tells the main idea.

**2 Why does the volcano seem to erupt?**

**A** The model volcano is very hot.

**B** Flour and water dry quickly.

**C** Vinegar and baking soda bubble and fizz when mixed.

**D** The volcano is shaped like a cone.

> **Tip**
> The directions do not give the answer to this question. Draw a conclusion by putting together information from the directions with your own knowledge.

**3 The purpose of this article is to**

**A** explain how to do something

**B** inform readers about types of model volcanoes

**C** persuade readers to make model volcanoes

**D** tell an entertaining story

**4 Where else might you find directions for making a model volcano?**

**A** an encyclopedia

**B** a science website for students

**C** a dictionary

**D** an atlas

**5 What would happen if you skipped Step 3?**

______________________________

______________________________

______________________________

> **Tip**
> Reread Step 1 and then Step 3. Would you be able to complete Step 3 without doing Step 2 first? Explain briefly the problem you would have.



| | |
|---|---|
| 1 | Ⓐ Ⓑ Ⓒ Ⓓ |
| 2 | Ⓐ Ⓑ Ⓒ Ⓓ |
| 3 | Ⓐ Ⓑ Ⓒ Ⓓ |
| 4 | Ⓐ Ⓑ Ⓒ Ⓓ |

Name ______________________________

## *Directions*

**Read this paragraph from a report that a student wrote about how chairs were invented. It has several mistakes that need correcting. Then answer Questions 6 through 8.**

> [1] Prehistoric people first sat on rocks. [2] Later, they begin to put wood on top of the rocks. [3] This arrangement became a type of seat. [4] After people invented tools. [5] They began to make furniture.

**6 Which sentence is the best topic sentence for the paragraph?**

**A** People have been building with rocks since ancient times.

**B** In some cultures, people squat or kneel.

**C** Modern furniture comes in a wide variety of styles.

**D** Chairs have a long and interesting history.

> **Tip**
> The topic sentence states the main idea of a paragraph. Which sentence expresses the main idea of this paragraph?

**7 Which is the best way to rewrite Sentence 2?**

**A** Later, they begins to put wood on top of the rocks.

**B** Later, they begun to put wood on top of the rocks.

**C** Later, they began to put wood on top of the rocks.

**D** Later, they beginning to put wood on top of the rocks.

**8 Which statement is a sentence fragment?**

**A** Statement 1

**B** Statement 2

**C** Statement 3

**D** Statement 4

> **Tip**
> Look for a dependent clause that cannot stand alone and should be combined into one sentence with the sentence that follows it.



| | |
|---|---|
| 6 | Ⓐ Ⓑ Ⓒ Ⓓ |
| 7 | Ⓐ Ⓑ Ⓒ Ⓓ |
| 8 | Ⓐ Ⓑ Ⓒ Ⓓ |

Name ________________________________________

## *Directions*

**Read the phrases. Look for an underlined word that contains an error in grammar. If all the underlined words are used correctly, mark "All correct."**

> **Tip**
> For each phrase, decide whether the underlined pronoun should be a subject pronoun or an object pronoun.

**9** **A** for us
**B** with them
**C** told Mark and I
**D** All correct

**10** **Which word in the sentence should be capitalized?**

**Our teacher asked us to read a magazine article about the planet mars.**

**A** teacher
**B** magazine
**C** planet
**D** mars

**11** **Choose the word that is spelled correctly and completes the sentence.**

**That was a funny ______ !**

**A** story
**B** storey
**C** storie
**D** storee

**12** **Write a sentence about a school science project. Use at least one subject pronoun or object pronoun. Write S above a subject pronoun and O above an object pronoun. Capitalize and punctuate correctly.**

> **Tip**
> Remember that a subject pronoun takes the place of one or more nouns in the subject of a sentence. An object pronoun follows an action verb or a preposition.

________________________________________

________________________________________

________________________________________

________________________________________

| | |
|---|---|
| 9 | Ⓐ Ⓑ Ⓒ Ⓓ |
| 10 | Ⓐ Ⓑ Ⓒ Ⓓ |
| 11 | Ⓐ Ⓑ Ⓒ Ⓓ |

STOP

Name ___________________________________________

## *Directions*

**Read the story below. Then answer Questions 1 through 5. You may look back at the story.**

# The Mystery Maps

Martine peered at the paper she had found under her door that morning. The paper was torn and had dotted lines and squiggly shapes. It looked like part of a treasure map.

Then Martine's friend Natasha called. "Hey, Martine," Natasha said. "I got some weird piece of paper under my door."

"I got one, too!" cried Martine.

"I think it's some kind of map," Natasha said. "My piece has a big X on it!"

"Mine has Alameda Street marked off!" Martine said.

Their friend Valerie had a map, too. Hers had Third Avenue marked. Soon, the three friends met at the corner of Third Avenue and Alameda Street. Their pieces of paper fit together like a jigsaw puzzle. Starting at the corner where they were, the girls followed a dotted line on the map. The line wound around trees, between bushes, and behind garages.

After a while, the three friends found themselves in a backyard with a picnic table. Just then the back door of the house opened, and a girl came out carrying a plate of muffins.

"My name is Annika," she said. "I'm visiting my aunt for the summer. I wanted to meet some girls in town, and I wanted to make it fun. My aunt said you three might enjoy solving a puzzle together. So we arranged this with your parents' help."

Martine laughed. "I thought we were going to find a treasure!"

"We did," Valerie said. "A new friend is a true treasure!"

**Tip**
Don't let the quotation marks and characters' names confuse you. If necessary, read more slowly to be sure you understand what is going on in the story.

**Tip**
Many of the sentences spoken by the characters end with exclamation marks. What does this tell you about how the characters feel?

**Tip**
How do you think the story will end? Making predictions as you read will help you enjoy and remember the story.

Name ______________________________

1 **The three friends in the story speak in a way that shows they are**

**A** upset
**B** jealous
**C** bored
**D** excited

2 **You can tell this story is a mystery because**

**A** it teaches a lesson
**B** it tells about real people and real events
**C** the action centers on finding the answer to a question
**D** the characters do things that real people would not do

> **Tip**
> Read all the choices before you mark your answer. Then pick the one that *best* describes a mystery.

3 **The girls meet at the corner of Third Avenue and Alameda Street because**

**A** it is close to all their houses
**B** those streets are shown on the map
**C** that is where their school is
**D** Martine's mother tells them to meet there

> **Tip**
> If you are not sure of the answer, go back and scan the story for the names of these streets.

4 **The words that best describe Annika are**

**A** friendly and clever
**B** lonesome and sad
**C** curious and excited
**D** shy and unsure of herself

> **Tip**
> If you are not sure which character is named Annika, look back at the story before you answer the question.

5 **Here are some events from the story. Place the events in order from 1 to 4 by writing the numbers in the boxes next to each sentence.**

☐ The three friends meet.
☐ Martine finds a paper.
☐ A girl comes out carrying muffins.
☐ The girls follow the dotted line.

| | |
|---|---|
| 1 | Ⓐ Ⓑ Ⓒ Ⓓ |
| 2 | Ⓐ Ⓑ Ⓒ Ⓓ |
| 3 | Ⓐ Ⓑ Ⓒ Ⓓ |
| 4 | Ⓐ Ⓑ Ⓒ Ⓓ |





GO ON

Name ______________________________

*Directions*

**Read this paragraph from a report that a student wrote about maps. It has several mistakes that need correcting. Then answer Questions 6 through 8.**

**Maps**

[1] There are many different kinds of maps. [2] Different kinds of maps are used for different purposes. [3] One kind of map helps drivers find out the names of roads and where the roads go. [4] Another kind of map show elevations, or how high or low the land is. [5] Mt. Everest is the highest mountain in the world. [6] Still other maps show the boundaries that people have decided upon to separate states or countries.

**6 Which sentence does not belong in the paragraph?**

**A** Sentence 3

**B** Sentence 4

**C** Sentence 5

**D** Sentence 6

> **Tip**
> The sentence that does not belong is the one that does not stay on the topic of the paragraph.

**7 Choose the best way to combine Sentences 1 and 2.**

**A** There are many different kinds of maps different kinds of maps are used for different purposes.

**B** There are many different kinds of maps, different kinds of maps are used for different purposes.

**C** There are many different kinds of maps that are used for different purposes.

**D** There are many different kinds of maps, different kinds of maps that are used for different purposes.

**8 Which is the best way to rewrite Sentence 4?**

**A** Another kind of map shows elevations, or how high or low the land is.

**B** Another kind of map's shows elevations, or how high or low the land is.

**C** Another kind of map show elevations, or how high or low the land's are.

**D** Another kind of map showing elevations, or how high or low the land is.

> **Tip**
> Read each answer choice carefully to be sure all the words are written correctly and all verbs agree with their subjects.



6 Ⓐ Ⓑ Ⓒ Ⓓ
7 Ⓐ Ⓑ Ⓒ Ⓓ
8 Ⓐ Ⓑ Ⓒ Ⓓ

Name ____________________

## *Directions*

**Look at the underlined part of the sentence. Choose the answer that shows the correct punctuation for that part. If the underlined part is correct, mark "Correct as is."**

**9** **"Your backpack is under my seat" Ling said to Dorian.**

**A** seat, Ling

**B** seat," Ling

**C** seat." Ling

**D** Correct as is

**10** **Which word best completes the analogy?**

***Read* is to *book* as ______ is to *TV*.**

**A** *show*

**B** *newspaper*

**C** *picture*

**D** *watch*

**Tip**
An analogy tells how different things are related. Think of how *read* is related to *book*. Then pick the answer choice that is related to *TV* in the same way.

**11** **Choose the word that is spelled correctly and completes the sentence.**

**Nina wrote a short ______.**

**A** paragraff

**B** parragraf

**C** parragraph

**D** paragraph

**12** **Write a sentence about making a new friend. Use at least one possessive pronoun. Circle the possessive pronoun. Capitalize and punctuate correctly.**

______________________________

______________________________

______________________________

**Tip**
Remember that a possessive pronoun shows ownership and takes the place of a possessive noun.



| | |
|---|---|
| 9 | Ⓐ Ⓑ Ⓒ Ⓓ |
| 10 | Ⓐ Ⓑ Ⓒ Ⓓ |
| 11 | Ⓐ Ⓑ Ⓒ Ⓓ |

STOP

Name ____________________

*Directions*

**Read the story below. Then answer Questions 1 through 5. You may look back at the story.**

# The Carved Mouse

There was once a king who collected carved animals. He had many carvings, but he had no carved mouse. So he asked two famous artists to come to the castle.

> **Tip**
> The first paragraph introduces the characters and sets the scene for the story. What do you think the king might ask the artists to do?

"Each of you must carve a mouse so lifelike and real that my cat will think it is alive. I will put them down together to see which mouse the cat jumps on. The artist who carves that mouse will get a bag of gold," the king explained.

One week later the carvers reappeared. The first carver had made a wooden mouse that was a perfect copy of a real mouse. The other carver had cut his mouse from a strange material. It didn't look at all like a real mouse.

"What's this?" said the king. "The wooden mouse is wonderful, but the other one will never fool my cat."

"Bring in the cat," said the second carver, "and let her decide which mouse is better."

When the cat came in, she jumped on the second carver's odd-looking mouse. She didn't even look at the wooden one.

> **Tip**
> As you read, make mental pictures of the characters and their actions. Doing so will help you understand and remember the events that take place in the story.

"You win," the surprised king told the second carver. "Now please tell me something. Why did the cat choose your work when it didn't even look like a real mouse?"

> **Tip**
> Predicting the outcome adds to your enjoyment and helps you understand the story. What answer do you think the second carver might give the king?

"I didn't carve my mouse from wood," the artist said. "I used dried fish."

The king laughed. "I'll have to give away two bags of gold," he said. "One goes to the artist who carved so well, and the other goes to the artist who carved so cleverly."

Name ______________________________

1 **The word *reappeared* in this story means**

A came back again

B will not return

C acts in a silly way

D without trying

> **Tip**
> Look for a familiar prefix, root word, and ending in the word *reappeared.* Combine the meanings of the word parts to figure out the meaning of the word.

2 **The cat chooses the second mouse because**

A many cats like to eat fish

B cats don't like wood

C it looks more lifelike

D the second mouse is closer to him

> **Tip**
> Use what you know about cats, as well as information from the story, to answer the question.

3 **Why does the king give away two bags of gold?**

A He thinks the first carver did a better job.

B He likes to give away gold.

C He dislikes the second carver.

D He thinks both carvers deserve a reward.

4 **Which sentence best expresses the main idea of this story?**

A A cat chooses an odd-looking mouse.

B A carver shows a king that cleverness can be as important as skill.

C Two artists carve two different kinds of mice.

D A king who collects carved animals decides to hold a contest.

5 **Write a sentence that tells how the king feels about the second carver at the end of the story.**

______________________________

______________________________

> **Tip**
> The question asks about the end of the story. Reread the ending and look for clues about how the king feels.



1 Ⓐ Ⓑ Ⓒ Ⓓ
2 Ⓐ Ⓑ Ⓒ Ⓓ
3 Ⓐ Ⓑ Ⓒ Ⓓ
4 Ⓐ Ⓑ Ⓒ Ⓓ

Name ____________________

## *Directions*

**Choose the sentence that best develops the topic sentence.**

**6** ***Cats are good pets for older people who live alone.***

**A** *Some people prefer to live alone, while others do not.*

**B** *Neighbors should check on older people from time to time.*

**C** *Cats are good companions and don't require a lot of care.*

**D** *Before you get a pet, you need to know how to take care of it.*

**Tip**
Think about the main idea expressed in the topic sentence. Choose the detail that gives more information about that idea.

**7** **What is the best pattern to use for organizing a passage that begins with this topic sentence?**

**A** cause and effect

**B** main idea and details

**C** sequence

**D** compare and contrast

**Tip**
Reread the topic sentence and the sentence you chose as your answer for Question 6. What pattern or text structure do you recognize?

**8** **The author probably wrote this sentence to**

**A** entertain readers with a story

**B** tell how to take care of a cat

**C** describe different kinds of cats

**D** persuade older people to get pet cats



| | |
|---|---|
| 6 | Ⓐ Ⓑ Ⓒ Ⓓ |
| 7 | Ⓐ Ⓑ Ⓒ Ⓓ |
| 8 | Ⓐ Ⓑ Ⓒ Ⓓ |

Name ______________________________

# *Directions*

**Read the sentence. Then choose the answer in which the word *cover* has the same meaning as it does in the sentence.**

**9 The author's name is on the <u>cover</u> of the book.**

**A** cover a great distance

**B** cover with a blanket

**C** under cover of darkness

**D** magazine cover

**10 Which word is the antonym of the underlined adjective?**

**The artist used a <u>sharp</u> knife to carve the wood.**

**A** painful

**B** dull

**C** short

**D** new

> **Tip**
> Think about the meaning of the underlined word. Then pick the word that has the opposite meaning.

**11 Read the phrases. Choose the phrase containing an underlined word that is spelled wrong. If all the underlined words are spelled correctly, mark "All correct."**

**A** dark <u>sunglasses</u>

**B** <u>pertect</u> from harm

**C** close your <u>eyes</u>

**D** All correct

**12 Write a sentence about an art project. Use at least two adjectives. Circle each adjective. Capitalize and punctuate correctly.**

______________________________

______________________________

______________________________

> **Tip**
> Remember that an adjective describes a noun or pronoun and may tell *what kind, how many,* or *which one.*

| | |
|---|---|
| 9 | Ⓐ Ⓑ Ⓒ Ⓓ |
| 10 | Ⓐ Ⓑ Ⓒ Ⓓ |
| 11 | Ⓐ Ⓑ Ⓒ Ⓓ |

STOP

Name ______________________________________________

*Directions*

**Read the story below. Then answer Questions 1 through 5. You may look back at the story.**

# Little Golden Hood

There was once a little girl who was called Little Golden Hood for the gold-colored cloak and hood she wore. One day, she set off to take a cake to her grandmother.

> **Tip**
> Does this story remind you of a familiar fairy tale? Read on to see how this story is like that one and how it is different.

Before long, she met a wolf. He asked in a friendly way where she was going. "I am taking a cake to Grandmother, who lives at the other side of the wood in the house near the windmill," Little Golden Hood told him.

The wolf took a shortcut through the wood to Grandmother's house. Grandmother was not at home, so the wolf let himself in, put on a nightcap, and climbed into bed.

> **Tip**
> How did the wolf know where Grandmother lived? Did you notice that Little Golden Hood told him in the paragraph before this?

A few minutes later, Little Golden Hood arrived. When she saw the wolf in the nightcap, she cried, "Grandmother, you look so much like Friend Wolf! What hairy arms you have!"

"All the better to hug you, my child," said the wolf.

"Grandmother, what great white teeth you have!"

"That's for crunching little children with!" The wolf opened his jaws wide. Little Golden Hood ducked, so all the wolf caught in his mouth was her hood. The wolf drew back, crying and shaking. The little golden hood had burned his tongue! You see, it was a magic hood that kept its wearer safe from harm.

The wolf, howling and yowling, ran for the door. Just then, Grandmother returned carrying a sack. She spread the sack across the door, and the wolf jumped right into it. Then Grandmother tied up the sack and threw it in the river.

Little Golden Hood never stopped to talk to a wolf again. In fine weather, early in the morning, you can still see her in the fields with her pretty little hood, the color of the sun.

> **Tip**
> As you read, ask yourself questions about the story. What might you see in the fields in fine weather early in the morning that is a golden color?

Name ____________________

1 **Which picture shows the meaning of the word *wood* as it used in this story?**

A

B

C

D

> **Tip**
> Scan the story for the word *wood*. Then reread that part of the story to figure out which meaning of *wood* is used.

2 **Why does the wolf put on Grandmother's nightcap?**

**A** to keep his head warm
**B** to play a trick on Grandmother
**C** to make Little Golden Hood think he is Grandmother
**D** so he can take a nap before Little Golden Hood arrives

3 **How might the outcome of the story change if Grandmother got home before the wolf arrived?**

**A** Grandmother might chase the wolf away before Little Golden Hood got there.
**B** The wolf might have gobbled up Little Golden Hood.
**C** Grandmother might make the wolf give back her nightcap.
**D** Little Golden Hood might go home instead of going to Grandmother's.

> **Tip**
> Picture the scene in your mind to help you decide which answer choice makes the most sense.

4 **The wolf cries out because**

**A** he opens his jaws too wide
**B** he swallows red-hot coals
**C** the golden hood burns him
**D** hot tea burns his tongue

5 **You could <u>best</u> predict what the wolf in this story might say and do by**

**A** comparing the story to other fairy tales
**B** knowing what wolves are like in real life
**C** thinking about what you would do in the same situation
**D** thinking about how this story is different from other stories you know

> **Tip**
> Several of the answer choices are useful strategies for making predictions. Ask yourself which one would work best for this particular story.

| | |
|---|---|
| 1 | Ⓐ Ⓑ Ⓒ Ⓓ |
| 2 | Ⓐ Ⓑ Ⓒ Ⓓ |
| 3 | Ⓐ Ⓑ Ⓒ Ⓓ |
| 4 | Ⓐ Ⓑ Ⓒ Ⓓ |
| 5 | Ⓐ Ⓑ Ⓒ Ⓓ |

Name ______________________________

*D*irections

**Read these notes that a student took for a report about butterflies. Then answer Questions 6 through 8.**

1. A butterfly's life begins when a female lays her eggs.
2. Next, a tiny caterpillar, or larva, hatches from the egg.
3. Finally, the cocoon splits apart, and the butterfly pulls itself out.
4. After the caterpillar grows to its full size, it builds a cocoon, or protective covering, around itself.

**6 How should the notes be organized before writing a first draft?**

**A** 1, 2, 3, 4

**B** 1, 3, 2, 4

**C** 1, 2, 4, 3

**D** 2, 1, 3, 4

**Tip**
Think about the sequence of events to put the notes in an order that makes sense.

**7 What is the best pattern to use for organizing this report?**

**A** main idea and details

**B** sequence

**C** cause and effect

**D** compare and contrast

**Tip**
Think about the way you organized the notes in Question 6 and the kinds of signal words you see in the sentences.

**8 The purpose of this report is to**

**A** retell a folktale about a butterfly

**B** describe the patterns of butterflies' wings

**C** inform readers about a butterfly's life cycle

**D** persuade readers to protect butterflies



| | |
|---|---|
| 6 | Ⓐ Ⓑ Ⓒ Ⓓ |
| 7 | Ⓐ Ⓑ Ⓒ Ⓓ |
| 8 | Ⓐ Ⓑ Ⓒ Ⓓ |

Name ______________________________

## *Directions*

**Choose the word or words that correctly complete the sentence.**

**9 The wolf's teeth were ______ than mine.**

**A** more bigger

**B** bigger

**C** biggest

**D** most biggest

**10 Look at the underlined part of the sentence. Choose the answer that shows the correct punctuation for that part. If the underlined part is correct, mark "Correct as is."**

**What an exciting day this has <u>been?</u>**

**A** been!

**B** been.

**C** been

**D** Correct as is

**11 Choose the word that is spelled correctly and completes the sentence.**

**These ______ are bright red.**

**A** berrys

**B** berryies

**C** berry's

**D** berries

> **Tip**
> Think about the spelling of the singular noun *berry*. Then recall how the spelling changes when the noun is plural.

**12 Write a sentence that uses at least one adjective to compare an animal with one or more other animals. Capitalize and punctuate correctly.**

______________________________

______________________________

______________________________

> **Tip**
> Use *-er* or *more* to compare one thing with another. Use *-est* or *most* to compare one thing with two or more other things.

| | |
|---|---|
| **9** | Ⓐ Ⓑ Ⓒ Ⓓ |
| **10** | Ⓐ Ⓑ Ⓒ Ⓓ |
| **11** | Ⓐ Ⓑ Ⓒ Ⓓ |

STOP

Name ________________________________

*Directions*

**Read the story below. Then answer Questions 1 through 5. You may look back at the story.**

# Aniz the Shepherd

## A Folktale from China

A wealthy landlord hired a boy named Aniz to watch his sheep. People liked Aniz and loved to hear him play his flute. The landlord, however, was constantly scolding Aniz. One day, the angry landlord smashed the flute to pieces. Aniz wandered through the streets with tears running down his face.

Soon he met an old man who made him a wonderful new flute and taught him how to play it. Now Aniz played tunes as sweet as the bees' sweetest honey. Even the animals of the forest would gather around and listen.

**Tip**
As you read, contrast the way the old man treats Aniz with the way the wealthy landlord treated him.

One night the landlord dreamed about a white rabbit with a black spot on its head. He told his sons that the one who brought him that rabbit would inherit all his wealth.

The first son went to the forest and saw many animals listening as Aniz played his flute. One was a white rabbit with a black spot. When the first son grabbed the rabbit, Aniz played louder. The rabbit kicked and wiggled and got free. The second son tried the next day, but the same thing happened. The third son had no better luck than his brothers.

**Tip**
First, Aniz plays louder. Then, the rabbit gets free. Think about how the two events might be related.

Finally, the wealthy landlord went to the forest himself. Aniz saw him and began to play his flute. The animals came and made a circle around the landlord. There were rabbits, bears, snakes, foxes, wolves, and other creatures.

"Please don't let them eat me!" the landlord begged. "I will give you anything you want!"

"Very well. I will spare your life," said Aniz. "But from now on, you must be kind to poor folk. When you get home, you must give half of your riches to the poor villagers."

**Tip**
Are you surprised by what Aniz wants from the landlord? What does his request tell you about the kind of person he is?

The landlord did as Aniz had said. Now the poor people of the village could buy good food and warm clothing, and Aniz was more popular than ever.

Name ______________________________

**1 This folktale is like other folktales because**

**A** it reflects the values of a culture

**B** the main character solves a mystery

**C** some of the events really happened

**D** a moral is stated at the end of the story

**Tip**

Think about the characteristics of folktales. Pick the answer that is true both for this folktale and for others.

**2 The old man treats Aniz**

**A** harshly

**B** obediently

**C** suspiciously

**D** kindly

**Tip**

Read the question carefully to be sure you understand which character it asks about. Two characters in the story treat Aniz in very different ways.

**3 What does the story mean when it says that Aniz "played tunes as sweet as the bees' sweetest honey"?**

**A** The new flute buzzed like a bee.

**B** Bees came to listen and got honey on the flute.

**C** The new flute had a beautiful sound.

**D** Aniz ate honey before he played the flute.

**4 The rabbit gets free because**

**A** he fights harder when Aniz plays louder

**B** the first son decides to let him go

**C** Aniz shouts at the first son

**D** the other animals help him

**Tip**

The cause and effect relationship between these events is not explained in the story. You can figure it out by eliminating answers that do not make sense.

**5 How does the landlord feel when the animals surround him? How can you tell?**

______________________________

______________________________

______________________________



| | |
|---|---|
| 1 | Ⓐ Ⓑ Ⓒ Ⓓ |
| 2 | Ⓐ Ⓑ Ⓒ Ⓓ |
| 3 | Ⓐ Ⓑ Ⓒ Ⓓ |
| 4 | Ⓐ Ⓑ Ⓒ Ⓓ |



GO ON

Name ______________________________

*Directions*

**Read this paragraph that a student wrote for a report about rabbits and hares. It has several mistakes that need correcting. Then answer Questions 6 through 8.**

**Rabbits and Hares**

[1] What is the difference between a rabbit and a hare. [2] One difference is that baby rabbits are born without fur, while baby hares are born with fur. [3] In general, hares are more larger than rabbits and have longer ears. [4] Most rabbits live in colonies with other rabbits most hares do not live in colonies.

**6 Which sentence contains two complete thoughts and should be written as two sentences?**

**A** Sentence 1

**B** Sentence 2

**C** Sentence 3

**D** Sentence 4

**7 Sentence 1 should end with ______ instead of a period.**

**A** an exclamation point

**B** a question mark

**C** a comma

**D** quotation marks

**Tip**
Think about the purpose of the sentence. Choose the end punctuation that is correct for this type of sentence.

**8 Which is the best way to rewrite Sentence 3?**

**A** In general, hares are larger than rabbits and have longer ears.

**B** In general, hares are more larger than rabbits and have more longer ears.

**C** In general, hares are largest than rabbits and have longest ears.

**D** In general, hares are larger than rabbits and have more longer ears.

**Tip**
Two adjectives are used in the sentence to compare hares and rabbits. Pick the answer in which both adjectives that compare are used correctly.



6 Ⓐ Ⓑ Ⓒ Ⓓ
7 Ⓐ Ⓑ Ⓒ Ⓓ
8 Ⓐ Ⓑ Ⓒ Ⓓ

Name ______________________________

## *Directions*

**Choose the words that correctly complete the sentence.**

**9 Josh _____ the flute because it _____ his favorite instrument.**

**A** play, are
**B** plays, is
**C** playing, is
**D** plays, being

> **Tip**
> Make sure that each verb in the sentence agrees with its subject.

**10 Look at the underlined part of the sentence. Choose the answer that shows the correct capitalization for that part. If the underlined part is correct, mark "Correct as is."**

**Our class publishes a newspaper called *The Hartley School news*.**

**A** *the Hartley School news*
**B** *the hartley school news*
**C** *The Hartley School News*
**D** Correct as is

**11 Read the phrases. Choose the phrase containing an underlined word that is spelled wrong. If all the underlined words are spelled correctly, mark "All correct."**

**A** in the country
**B** usualy on time
**C** hopped on one foot
**D** a peaceful morning

> **Tip**
> Remember that a verb can express action or being.

**12 Write a sentence about music or a musical instrument. Use two verbs in the sentence and circle the verbs. Capitalize and punctuate correctly.**

______________________________

______________________________

______________________________

| | |
|---|---|
| 9 | Ⓐ Ⓑ Ⓒ Ⓓ |
| 10 | Ⓐ Ⓑ Ⓒ Ⓓ |
| 11 | Ⓐ Ⓑ Ⓒ Ⓓ |

STOP

Name ________________________________________

*Directions*

**WRITE A STORY** Think about someone you know or have heard about who used creativity to solve a problem. Write a story that tells how a character resolves a problem or conflict in a creative way.

Use the story map below to plan your story, and write it on a separate sheet of paper. When you are finished with the draft, use the Writer's Checklist to revise and edit your work. Then make a final copy of your story.

**Characters**

**Setting**

**Beginning**

**Middle**

**Ending**

Name ______________________________

## *Writer's Checklist*

- ❑ Do you begin by introducing your characters and setting?
- ❑ Do you explain your main character's problem and how it began?
- ❑ Do you show how the main character used creativity to resolve the problem or conflict?
- ❑ Did you include interesting words and details?
- ❑ Did you include different types of sentences?
- ❑ Do you have any run-on sentences or fragments?
- ❑ Did you begin sentences and names of people with capital letters?
- ❑ Did you end every sentence with an end mark?
- ❑ Did you use correct punctuation for quotations?
- ❑ Did you try to spell each word correctly?





STOP

Name ____________________

*Directions*

**Read the article below. Then answer Questions 1 through 5. You may look back at the article.**

# The Secret Life of a Supermarket

It takes many workers to keep a supermarket running smoothly. Goods flow constantly in and out of the market. As shoppers make their selections, the items must be replaced.

## Supermarket Workers

Stock clerks put items on the shelves. They code the prices into the store computer and make sure the prices are visible on the shelves.

Meat workers prepare packages of meat and fish under sanitary conditions. They wrap each package in plastic to seal out air and germs. Then they place it on a scale. Finally, they attach a label that tells the kind of meat it is, the weight, and the price.

> **Tip**
> This article is divided into sections that are labeled with headings. Use the headings to help you identify the main idea of each section.

## Finding Your Way Around

Shoppers have many ways to find the items they want. In large supermarkets, the aisles have signs that show the aisle number and the kinds of products found there. Some supermarkets have a directory on the shopping carts. Of course, shoppers can also ask a store worker.

A supermarket usually has a section for fruits and vegetables, a dairy department with refrigerated cases, and a frozen food department. In addition, many supermarkets sell greeting cards, magazines, and other items. Some supermarkets have ATM machines that make it easier for shoppers to get cash.

> **Tip**
> Notice how the information in each section is organized. Possible types of structure include main idea and details, cause and effect, sequence, and compare and contrast.

## Checkout

After shoppers find what they need, they take the items to the checkout counter. First, the cashier looks for a bar code, a set of thin and thick black lines that can be read by the store computer. A laser scans the bar code, and the computer then sends price information to that cash register. Finally, the cashier tells the total, and a packer puts the items into bags. With the help of supermarket workers, the shopping is done!

> **Tip**
> This section is organized differently from the others. Look for signal words that give you a clue about how the text is structured.

Name ______________________________

1 **This article is an example of**

**A** realistic fiction

**B** a biography

**C** a persuasive essay

**D** expository nonfiction

2 **Which of these is <u>not</u> a way for shoppers to find the goods they need?**

**A** using a directory on a shopping cart

**B** asking a store worker

**C** using an ATM machine

**D** looking for signs in each aisle

> **Tip**
> Pay attention to the key word *not*. If you are not sure which answer is correct, reread the appropriate section to see which choice is *not* mentioned there.

3 **Which sentence expresses the main idea of the section "Finding Your Way Around"?**

**A** Some supermarkets have a directory on the shopping carts.

**B** A supermarket usually has a section for fruits and vegetables, a dairy department with refrigerated cases, and a frozen food department.

**C** Shoppers have many ways to find the items they want.

**D** Some supermarkets have ATM machines that make it easier for shoppers to get cash.

> **Tip**
> All of the answer choices are sentences found in the section, but only one of them expresses the main idea of the section.

4 **The "Checkout" section of the article is organized according to**

**A** main idea and details

**B** sequence

**C** cause and effect

**D** compare and contrast

5 **Write a sentence that tells the main idea of this article.**

______________________________

______________________________

______________________________

1 Ⓐ Ⓑ Ⓒ Ⓓ
2 Ⓐ Ⓑ Ⓒ Ⓓ
3 Ⓐ Ⓑ Ⓒ Ⓓ
4 Ⓐ Ⓑ Ⓒ Ⓓ

Name ______________________________

## *Directions*

**Read this paragraph that a student wrote about an oil spill. Then answer Questions 6 through 8.**

**The Worst Oil Spill**

[1] In 1989, a supertanker was shipwrecked off the coast of Alaska. [2] It took three years, more than 11,000 people, and over two billion dollars to clean up most of that oil. [3] It was the worst oil spill in the history of North America.

**6 Where would this sentence best fit in the paragraph?**

**More than ten million gallons of heavy black oil spilled into the waters of Prince William Sound.**

**A** before Sentence 1

**B** before Sentence 2

**C** before Sentence 3

**D** after Sentence 3

**Tip**
Try rereading the paragraph and adding the sentence in different places. Where does it sound right to you?

**7 Which of these sentences tells more about the main idea of the paragraph?**

**A** Oil is used to heat homes and to manufacture products such as gasoline.

**B** People helped by cleaning the beaches and oil-soaked animals.

**C** The capital of Alaska is Juneau.

**D** Shipwrecks can be caused by storms, poor visibility, and human error.

**8 What source did the student probably use to find this information?**

**A** yesterday's newspaper

**B** the website of a local oil company

**C** a newspaper article from 1989

**D** an encyclopedia

**Tip**
Scan the article and think about the kind of information it contains. Then think about the kind of information that you might find in each of the resources named in the answer choices.



| | |
|---|---|
| 6 | Ⓐ Ⓑ Ⓒ Ⓓ |
| 7 | Ⓐ Ⓑ Ⓒ Ⓓ |
| 8 | Ⓐ Ⓑ Ⓒ Ⓓ |

Name ______________________________

## *Directions*

**Choose the word that correctly completes the sentence.**

**9 Our friends _______ come to help us.**

**A** has

**B** have

**C** is

**D** are

**10 Look at the underlined part of the sentence. Choose the answer that shows the correct punctuation for that part. If the underlined part is correct, mark "Correct as is."**

**When his sister's bicycle chain <u>came off Jeff</u> wanted to help.**

**A** came off, Jeff

**B** came off Jeff,

**C** came off. Jeff

**D** Correct as is

**11 Choose the word that is spelled correctly and completes the sentence.**

**Mike _______ forgot his wallet.**

**A** carelissly

**B** cairlessly

**C** carelessly

**D** cairlissie

> **Tip**
> Think about the correct spelling of the root word and of the suffixes that are added to it.

**12 Write a sentence about a visit to a supermarket. Use a helping verb in the sentence. Write H above the helping verb and M above the main verb. Capitalize and punctuate correctly.**

> **Tip**
> Remember that a helping verb comes before the main verb and that another word may sometimes come between the helping verb and the main verb.

______________________________

______________________________

______________________________

| | |
|---|---|
| 9 | Ⓐ Ⓑ Ⓒ Ⓓ |
| 10 | Ⓐ Ⓑ Ⓒ Ⓓ |
| 11 | Ⓐ Ⓑ Ⓒ Ⓓ |

STOP

Name ______________________________

*Directions*

**Read the story below. Then answer Questions 1 through 5. You may look back at the story.**

# Living on Elm Street

Steven lives in Manchester, New Hampshire. The main street is called Elm Street. One day, Steven went looking for elm trees on Elm Street. When he didn't find any, he went to visit Mrs. Sanchez. She had lived on Elm Street for many years.

> **Tip**
> As you read, ask questions that will help you understand the story. For example, why aren't there any elm trees on Elm Street? Read on to find the answer.

"The elm trees were gone long before you were born," Mrs. Sanchez told Steven. "A hurricane blew most of them down in 1938. Several years later Dutch Elm Disease made the rest of the trees sick."

"That's too bad," said Steven. "What were they like?"

"They were just beautiful," said Mrs. Sanchez. "Some were 100 feet high! They formed a canopy over the entire street. Walking down the street was like walking under an umbrella."

Steven was quiet for a minute. It seemed very sad that these beautiful trees were gone. "Do you think we'll ever have elm trees on Elm Street again?" he asked quietly.

Mrs. Sanchez smiled. "It's funny that you should ask that." She handed Steven a letter. "Go ahead, read it," she said.

> **Tip**
> As you read, make predictions about what may happen next. Why do you think Mrs. Sanchez is smiling?

The letter was from the city of Manchester. It described two new kinds of elm trees, the New Harmony and the Valley Forge, that could not get Dutch Elm Disease. Government scientists had worked for twenty years to develop these trees, and now they were ready to be planted. The city of Manchester wanted to know if Mrs. Sanchez wanted an elm tree in her yard again.

Steven handed Mrs. Sanchez back her letter. "Which kind will you plant?" he asked with a smile.

> **Tip**
> Think about Steven's question. He doesn't ask whether Mrs. Sanchez will accept the offer. He asks what kind of tree she wants. Why is he so sure she wants an elm tree?

His neighbor laughed. "One of each, of course."

Name ______________________________

**1 The author's main purpose for writing this article was probably to**

**A** entertain readers with a pleasant story

**B** give information about the elm trees in Manchester

**C** persuade people to plant elm trees

**D** tell about events in the life of Mrs. Sanchez

> **Tip**
> Eliminate answer choices that would not qualify as the author's main purpose until you are left with only one.

**2 Here are some events from the story. Place the events in order from 1 to 4 by writing the numbers in the boxes next to each sentence.**

☐ Steven reads Mrs. Sanchez's letter from the city.

☐ A hurricane blows down the elm trees.

☐ Steven goes looking for elm trees on Elm Street.

☐ Elm trees form a canopy on Elm Street.

> **Tip**
> Think carefully about the order that makes sense. Not all of these events happened in the same order as they are told about in the story.

**3 Which statement is an opinion?**

**A** Elm trees can grow to be 100 feet tall.

**B** Years ago Elm Street in Manchester was lined with elm trees.

**C** Scientists developed new types of elm trees.

**D** It was sad when Manchester's elm trees died.

**4 Steven is so sure about how Mrs. Sanchez will feel because**

**A** she has fond memories of the elm trees

**B** he has known her all his life

**C** she loves getting things for free

**D** he read what she wrote in her letter

**5 Replanting elm trees in Manchester is similar to**

**A** buying a new kind of rose bush

**B** bringing endangered animals back into the wild

**C** planting a large vegetable garden

**D** harvesting a crop of apples

> **Tip**
> The question asks about returning elm trees to where they had been before. Which answer choice describes a similar activity?



| | |
|---|---|
| 1 | Ⓐ Ⓑ Ⓒ Ⓓ |
| 3 | Ⓐ Ⓑ Ⓒ Ⓓ |
| 4 | Ⓐ Ⓑ Ⓒ Ⓓ |
| 5 | Ⓐ Ⓑ Ⓒ Ⓓ |

Name ______________________________

# *Directions*

**Read this paragraph from a report that a student wrote about fireworks. Then answer Questions 6 through 8.**

> **Fireworks Facts**
>
> [1] Fireworks as we know them contain ingredients that make an explosion and make color. [2] The materials in fireworks that cause the explosion include powdered saltpeter, sulfur, and charcoal. [3] Other powdered materials are added to produce different colors. [4] Copper is used for blue. [5] Sodium is used for yellow.

**6 Choose the best way to combine Sentences 4 and 5.**

**A** Copper is used for blue, and sodium is used for yellow.
**B** Copper is used for blue sodium is used for yellow.
**C** Copper and sodium are used, they are used for blue and yellow.
**D** Copper is used for blue, sodium being used for yellow.

> **Tip**
> Choose the sentence that sounds best and is punctuated correctly.

**7 The student probably wrote this paragraph to**

**A** encourage readers to see a fireworks display
**B** describe the beauty of a fireworks display
**C** tell a tall tale about fireworks
**D** give information about how fireworks are made

**8 Which of these is the best source for finding out what the word *sulfur* means?**

**A** an encyclopedia
**B** a thesaurus
**C** a dictionary
**D** an atlas

> **Tip**
> Notice that the question asks about finding the meaning of a word, not about finding facts about sulfur.



| | |
|---|---|
| 6 | Ⓐ Ⓑ Ⓒ Ⓓ |
| 7 | Ⓐ Ⓑ Ⓒ Ⓓ |
| 8 | Ⓐ Ⓑ Ⓒ Ⓓ |

Name ______________________________

## *Directions*

**Choose the word that correctly completes the sentence.**

**9 The trees ______ tall and beautiful before the wind knocked them down.**

**A** was

**B** are

**C** were

**D** is

> **Tip**
> Read the whole sentence before you pick your answer. Notice the tense of the verb *knocked* later in the sentence.

**10 Look at the underlined part of the sentence. Choose the answer that shows the correct capitalization for that part. If the underlined part is correct, mark "Correct as is."**

**The Hernandez children lived on Elm Street.**

**A** hernandez children

**B** hernandez Children

**C** Hernandez Children

**D** Correct as is

**11 Read the phrases. Choose the phrase containing an underlined word that is spelled wrong. If all the underlined words are spelled correctly, mark "All correct."**

**A** write a letter

**B** sit hear

**C** father and son

**D** All correct

> **Tip**
> Homophones, such as *right* and *write, hear* and *hear,* or *son* and *sun,* sound the same but are spelled differently. Is the homophone in each phrase correct?

**12 Write two sentences about trees. Use an action verb in the first sentence and a linking verb in the second sentence. Capitalize and punctuate correctly.**

______________________________

______________________________

______________________________



| | |
|---|---|
| 9 | Ⓐ Ⓑ Ⓒ Ⓓ |
| 10 | Ⓐ Ⓑ Ⓒ Ⓓ |
| 11 | Ⓐ Ⓑ Ⓒ Ⓓ |

STOP

Name ________________________________

*Directions*

**Read the article below. Then answer Questions 1 through 5. You may look back at the article.**

# A Giant in the Forest

What is the largest living thing in the world? Is it an elephant? Is it a whale? Actually, the world's largest living thing is not an animal at all. It is a tree called the sequoia that grows in the mountains of California. You can find it high up in the Sierra Nevada range.

**Tip**
From the title, you might think that this passage is a tale about a giant. Read the first few sentences to get a better idea of what the passage is about.

The largest sequoia tree is called the General Sherman tree. It is 101 feet around at its base and 272 feet tall. It is estimated to weigh more than 6,100 tons. The huge General Sherman tree is also ancient. It is thought to be 3,000 to 4,000 years old.

**Tip**
Use the numbers to create a mental picture of this huge tree. Keep in mind their great size as you continue reading.

Scientists believe there were many types of sequoia trees long ago, most of which became extinct during the Ice Age. Only three types are still found in the world today. Two of these—the giant sequoia and coast redwood—are found only in California. The other is the dawn redwood of southwestern China.

European settlers in the United States first saw sequoia trees in the 1850s. A hunter named Augustus T. Dowd was perhaps the first to see the huge trees. He was in the woods near a town named Murphy's Camp when he found a tree that was 24 feet in diameter. The tree was cut down in 1853. It took five men 22 days to cut through it. You can still see the gigantic stump of this tree in Calaveras Big Trees State Park.

**Tip**
As you read, notice how the author has organized the information.

Many people were upset that the huge trees were cut down. These people worked to make sure that the sequoias would be protected. One of the first wilderness preserves was set aside in 1864 to save the sequoias.

In 1890, Sequoia National Park, home of the General Sherman tree, was established. Many sequoias today are in parks, but some are still being cut down. Concerned people are working to preserve these ancient, beautiful trees for future generations.

**Tip**
Don't try to memorize the dates. Just read the paragraphs quickly to get a sense of how the trees have been protected.

Name ______________________________

1 **Why is the weight of the General Sherman tree given as an estimate?**

**A** It keeps growing.

**B** There is no way to determine its exact weight.

**C** The scale broke when scientists tried to weigh it.

**D** The author didn't want to bother looking up the information.

> **Tip**
> Use your own knowledge and common sense to figure out the answer to this question.

2 **The information in the second paragraph of the article is organized according to**

**A** main idea and details

**B** sequence of events

**C** cause and effect

**D** comparison and contrast

3 **The information in the last three paragraphs of the passage, beginning with the words *European settlers* . . . is organized according to**

**A** main idea and details

**B** sequence of events

**C** cause and effect

**D** comparison and contrast

> **Tip**
> To answer this question, think about your answer to question 3. Knowing how a selection is organized can help you locate information.

4 **To recall what people are doing to save sequoia trees today, you should reread**

**A** the whole article

**B** the beginning of the article

**C** the middle of the article

**D** the end of the article

5 **Write a statement that tells what the author believes about efforts to preserve the sequoias.**

> **Tip**
> First identify the author's opinion or viewpoint regarding sequoias. Then write a sentence that expresses that opinion.

______________________________

______________________________

______________________________



1 Ⓐ Ⓑ Ⓒ Ⓓ
2 Ⓐ Ⓑ Ⓒ Ⓓ
3 Ⓐ Ⓑ Ⓒ Ⓓ
4 Ⓐ Ⓑ Ⓒ Ⓓ

GO ON

Name ______________________________

*Directions*

**Read this paragraph from a report that a student wrote about lilies. It has several mistakes that need correcting. Then answer Questions 6 through 8.**

**Lilies**

[1] The lily is a wonderful garden plant. [2] There are about 200 varieties. [3] Choosing among them is difficult. [4] Lilies are a great favorite with florists because of they're strong stems, rich colors, and long-lasting blooms. [5] In addition, many lilies produce delicious fragrances.

**6 Which of these would be the best closing sentence for the paragraph?**

- **A** Thanks to its beauty and variety, this special flower has earned its popularity.
- **B** If you love flowers, think about becoming a florist.
- **C** You may see other kinds of lilies growing wild in the woods or fields.
- **D** Whether you choose flowers or vegetables, gardening is a great hobby.

**Tip**
Some of the sentences use words from the paragraph but do not tell about the main idea. Remember that the last sentence of a paragraph sometimes restates the main idea.

**7 Choose the best way to combine Sentences 2 and 3.**

- **A** There are about 200 varieties, choosing among them is difficult.
- **B** However there are about 200 varieties, choosing among them is difficult.
- **C** There are about 200 varieties, so choosing among them is difficult.
- **D** There are about 200 varieties choosing among them is difficult.

**8 The word *they're* in Sentence 4 should be replaced by ______.**

- **A** their
- **B** there
- **C** it's
- **D** its

**Tip**
Reread Sentence 4 to find the error. Think of how to correct the error before you look at the answers. Then look to see if your answer is one of the choices.



| | |
|---|---|
| 6 | Ⓐ Ⓑ Ⓒ Ⓓ |
| 7 | Ⓐ Ⓑ Ⓒ Ⓓ |
| 8 | Ⓐ Ⓑ Ⓒ Ⓓ |

Name ______________________________

## *Directions*

**Look at the underlined part of the sentence. Choose the answer that shows the correct punctuation for that part. If the underlined part is correct, mark "Correct as is."**

**9** **Tomatoes and corn, grow in the vegetable garden.**

A Tomatoes and corn grow

B Tomatoes, and corn grow

C Tomatoes and, corn grow

D Correct as is

> **Tip**
> Think about reasons for using commas. Is there any reason that this sentence needs a comma?

**10** **Choose the words that correctly complete the sentence.**

**When the wind ______, the tall trees ______.**

A blow, bend

B blow, bends

C blows, bend

D blows, bends

> **Tip**
> Make sure that each verb agrees with its subject. When a noun subject ends in *s*, the verb that agrees with it usually does not end in *s*.

**11** **Choose the word that is spelled correctly and completes the sentence.**

**Let's work ______ to solve this problem.**

A togather

B toogether

C togethar

D together

**12** **Write a sentence in the present tense about a tree or other plant that grows near your home. Be sure each verb agrees with its subject. Capitalize and punctuate correctly.**

______________________________

______________________________

______________________________

| | |
|---|---|
| 9 | Ⓐ Ⓑ Ⓒ Ⓓ |
| 10 | Ⓐ Ⓑ Ⓒ Ⓓ |
| 11 | Ⓐ Ⓑ Ⓒ Ⓓ |

STOP

Name ______________________________

*Directions*

**Read the story below. Then answer Questions 1 through 5. You may look back at the story.**

# The After-School Club

Billy belonged to an after-school club. The purpose was to have fun while learning something new. Each week, a different member planned and ran the meeting. This week it was Billy's turn. He had everyone sit around a table. Then he dumped the contents of a large paper bag onto the table. All the members looked with interest at the variety of items in front of them.

**Tip**
You can tell from the first paragraph that this story is probably realistic fiction. You can also get an idea of what the story is about.

"You have two minutes to memorize as many items as you can," Billy said. Everyone stared hard at the objects until Billy announced that time was up and returned the items to the bag. Then he asked how many items they remembered.

"I remember scissors, a spoon, a sugar cube, and a strainer," said Jan. "I memorized things that began with the same letter."

**Tip**
You don't have to keep track of the items that each student mentions. Instead, notice how each student remembers a different set of items.

"I remember an apple, a cup, a glove, a map, a rope, and a watch," said Lottie. "I tried to put things in alphabetical order."

"I remember the scissors and the knife, the thread and the rope, and the cup and the glass," said Mark. "I tried to think of things that were alike in some way."

"I remember the glove, the rope, the apple, the strainer, and the scissors," said Rick. "I used the first letters of some of the things to make a word—grass."

"Each of you had a different trick that helped you remember what you saw," said Billy. "I'll bet there are even more memory tricks that we should find out about!"

**Tip**
The word *trick* has more than one meaning. How is it used here?

The members all agreed that Billy's club meeting was one of the best they'd ever had. The following week would be Margie's turn. She had planned to tell jokes and riddles. Now she decided to do something that would better fit the purpose of the club.

Name ______________________________

1 **The word *trick* is used in this story to mean**

**A** something done to fool someone
**B** an act meant to annoy or injure
**C** a special skill or way of doing something
**D** a practical joke

**Tip**
Scan the story to find the word *trick*. Then reread the sentence to see what meaning of the word is used in the story.

2 **Which picture shows the items that a student remembered by thinking of things that are alike?**

**A** 

**B** 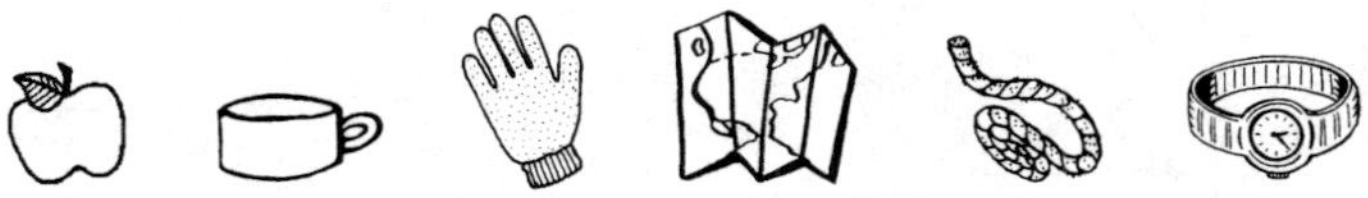

**C** 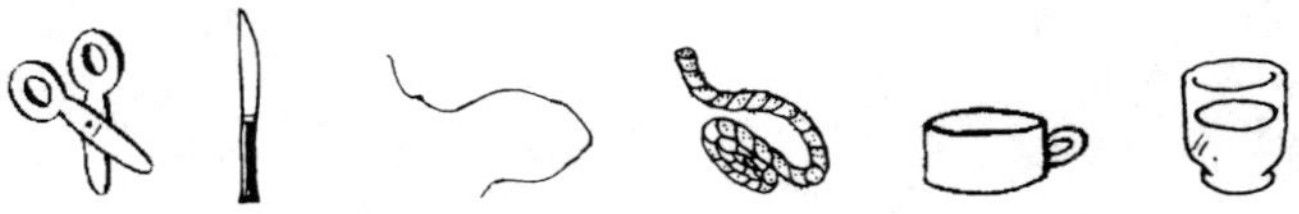

**D** 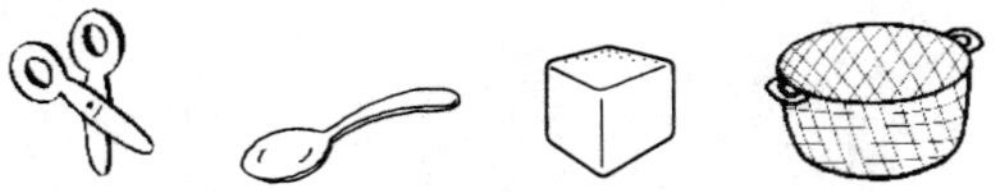

3 **When Rick uses the names of items to spell a word, he has to**

**A** alphabetize the names
**B** use the names of the largest items first
**C** figure out how the items are alike
**D** use the first letter of each item's name

**Tip**
Reread the part of the story about Rick's memory trick and how it works. Find that part of the story by looking for the name *Rick*.

4 **Margie changes her mind about what she will do because she**

**A** doesn't know enough jokes
**B** thinks Billy's idea is a good learning experience
**C** feels shy
**D** doesn't have enough time to get ready

**Tip**
Think about the details the author includes in the story. Ask yourself what these details show about how the author feels.

5 **Which statement best expresses the author's perspective?**

**A** You can learn and have fun at the same time.
**B** All students should belong to clubs.
**C** Having fun is more important than learning.
**D** Clubs are not a good way for students to spend their time.

1 Ⓐ Ⓑ Ⓒ Ⓓ
2 Ⓐ Ⓑ Ⓒ Ⓓ
3 Ⓐ Ⓑ Ⓒ Ⓓ
4 Ⓐ Ⓑ Ⓒ Ⓓ
5 Ⓐ Ⓑ Ⓒ Ⓓ



GO ON

Name ______________________________

*Directions*

**Read this paragraph that students wrote for a group project, and look at the graph they made. Then answer Questions 6 through 8.**

> **Movie Attendance Survey**
>
> Our group did a survey to find out how often people go to the movies. We asked 50 of our friends and relatives. Here are the results of our survey.

**Movie Attendance**

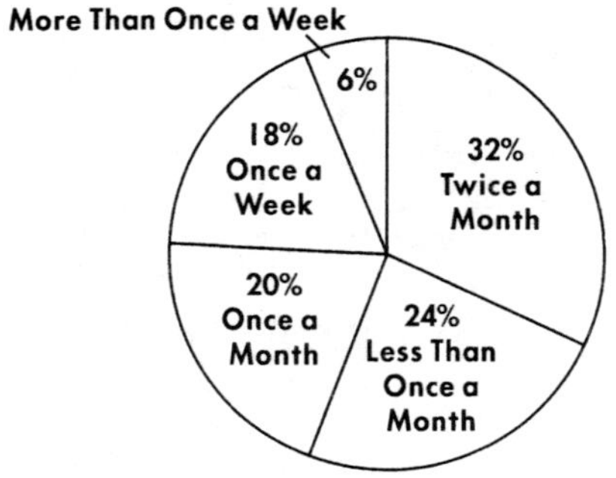


**6 According to the circle graph, how often do most people go to the movies?**

**A** once a week

**B** once a month

**C** twice a month

**D** more than twice a week

> **Tip**
> The key phrase in this question is *according to the circle graph*. This tells you to use the graph to find the answer.

**7 What information is found in the paragraph but <u>not</u> in the circle graph?**

**A** Few people go to the movies more than once a week.

**B** Of those surveyed, 20% said they go to the movies once a month.

**C** A total of 50 people were interviewed for the survey.

**D** Fewer people go to the movies once a month than twice a month.

**8 The circle graph shows you**

**A** how frequently people go to the movies

**B** what types of movies are most popular

**C** how many people go to movies and why they go

**D** why people of different ages like different movies

> **Tip**
> Take another look at the graph. Does it tell anything about the types of movies people like or why they go to the movies? Pick the answer that tells only what the graph shows.

6 Ⓐ Ⓑ Ⓒ Ⓓ
7 Ⓐ Ⓑ Ⓒ Ⓓ
8 Ⓐ Ⓑ Ⓒ Ⓓ

Name ______________________________

## *Directions*

**Choose the words that correctly complete the sentence.**

**9 We _____ good-bye when the ship _____.**

**A** wave, sailed

**B** waved, sailed

**C** waved, will sail

**D** will wave, sailed

> **Tip**
> A writer should not change tenses unless it is necessary. Use the same tense for both verbs in the sentence.

**10 Which word best completes the analogy?**

***Hand* is to *glove* as *foot* is to _____.**

**A** *walk*

**B** *toe*

**C** *fist*

**D** *shoe*

> **Tip**
> An analogy tells how different things are related. Think of how *hand* is related to *glove*. Then pick the answer choice that is related to *foot* in the same way.

**11 Choose the word that is spelled correctly and completes the sentence.**

**Take _____ time and don't rush.**

**A** you're

**B** your

**C** you'r

**D** youre

**12 Write two sentences about remembering things. Write the first sentence in the past tense and the second sentence in the future tense. Capitalize and punctuate correctly.**

______________________________

______________________________

______________________________



| | |
|---|---|
| 9 | Ⓐ Ⓑ Ⓒ Ⓓ |
| 10 | Ⓐ Ⓑ Ⓒ Ⓓ |
| 11 | Ⓐ Ⓑ Ⓒ Ⓓ |

STOP

Name ______________________________

*Directions*

**Read the article below. Then answer Questions 1 through 5. You may look back at the article.**

# An Artist's Story

> **Tip**
> From the title and first few sentences of the passage, you should be able to identify the genre.

Sculptor Luis Jimenez was born in 1940 in El Paso, Texas. At the age of six, he began helping in his father's neon sign workshop. Luis learned many skills. By the time he was sixteen years old, he could make glass, weld metal, and work tin.

Young Luis learned about art in other ways, too. He read books and visited museums. On visits to Mexico, his family's original homeland, he saw large murals painted by famous artists such as José Clemente Orozco. His experiences in Mexico gave Luis pride in his heritage and influenced his art work.

> **Tip**
> As you read, notice the dates and other signal words for sequence. What does this tell you about the way the information in this passage is organized?

In 1964, Luis earned a degree in art at the University of Texas. He has said that college gave him a chance to see and study things he would otherwise not have known about.

In his early years as an artist, Luis found that some people did not appreciate his favorite subject matter. He was told that serious artists did not work with subjects such as cowboys, Native Americans, and horses. To Luis, however, these images were important and worthwhile.

From 1966 to 1972, Luis lived and worked in New York City. There he began creating very large and lifelike fiberglass sculptures. His first one-person exhibition, held in New York in 1969, was a great success. After that, he was able for the first time to support himself through his art. Eventually, Luis returned to his home in the Southwest. He now lives and works in a former schoolhouse in New Mexico.

Luis Jimenez has received many awards and honors for his work. His large public sculptures can be seen in cities all over the United States. His most famous sculpture is called *Vaquero*, which means "cowboy." Another of his sculptures, a 32-foot-tall mustang, or wild horse, will be displayed at Denver International Airport. Today, nobody tells him that cowboys, Native Americans, and horses are not appropriate subjects for serious art.

> **Tip**
> How tall are you? Compare your own height to the height of a 32-foot-tall sculpture. Use this comparison to create a mental picture of the horse sculpture.

Name ________________________________________

**1 This article is an example of**

A realistic fiction

B a biography

C historical fiction

D a folktale

**2 The information in this passage is organized according to**

A main idea and details

B cause and effect

C comparison and contrast

D sequence of events

**3 Which activity is <u>not</u> mentioned in the article as a way that Luis learned about art?**

A reading books

B working in his father's shop

C painting murals in school

D visiting Mexico

**Tip**
Pay attention to the word *not.* Reread the first part of the article to recall how Luis learned about art. The correct answer is the activity that is *not* mentioned.

**4 You can tell from the article that *fiberglass* is**

A a material that can be used for sculptures

B a wild horse

C found only in the Southwest

D used in neon sign shops

**Tip**
If you are not sure what this word means, locate it in the article and use the context to decide which meaning makes sense.

**5 Choose <u>three</u> important events from Luis Jimenez's life. List them in the order in which they happened.**

(1) ________________________________________

(2) ________________________________________

(3) ________________________________________

**Tip**
Look back at the article to recall the correct order of the events you have chosen. Use clues such as dates and time order words to determine the sequence.

| | |
|---|---|
| 1 | Ⓐ Ⓑ Ⓒ Ⓓ |
| 2 | Ⓐ Ⓑ Ⓒ Ⓓ |
| 3 | Ⓐ Ⓑ Ⓒ Ⓓ |
| 4 | Ⓐ Ⓑ Ⓒ Ⓓ |





GO ON

Name ______________________________

## Directions

**Look at these dictionary entries. Then answer Questions 6 through 8.**

> **sculpt** (skulpt) *v.* 1. To create sculpture
>
> **sculp•tor** (skulp′ tər) *n.* An artist who creates sculptures
>
> **sculp•ture** (skulp′ chər) *n.* 1. The art of creating shapes or statues from stone, metal, clay, or other materials. 2. A work of art made by carving, chiseling, molding, or shaping. *v.* 3. To sculpt. 4. To decorate with sculpture.

**6 Which meaning of *sculpture* is used in the sentence below?**

**There is a sculpture of a swan near the pond in the park.**

**A** meaning 1
**B** meaning 2
**C** meaning 3
**D** meaning 4

> **Tip**
> Notice that *sculpture* can be used as a noun or as a verb. Decide how it is used in the sentence to help narrow your choices.

**7 Choose the word that correctly completes the sentence.**

**The __________ showed us some of her work.**

**A** sculpt
**B** sculptor
**C** sculpture
**D** sculptures

**8 Which guide words might you find at the top of a dictionary page with entries for *sculpt*, *sculptor*, and *sculpture*?**

**A** scramble—scuff
**B** scurry—seagull
**C** scaffold—scare
**D** scrutiny—scythe

> **Tip**
> Check the first few letters of the guide words and the entries. The entries should come between the guide words in alphabetical order.



| | |
|---|---|
| 6 | Ⓐ Ⓑ Ⓒ Ⓓ |
| 7 | Ⓐ Ⓑ Ⓒ Ⓓ |
| 8 | Ⓐ Ⓑ Ⓒ Ⓓ |

Name ______________________________

# *Directions*

**Choose the words that correctly complete the sentence.**

**9 Rita ______ a long time before she ______ a name for her new kitten.**

**A** thinked, choosed

**B** thinked, chose

**C** thought, choosed

**D** thought, chose

> **Tip**
> *Think* and *choose* are examples of irregular verbs. What do you know about the past tense of an irregular verb?

**10 Look at the underlined part of the sentence. Choose the answer that shows the correct punctuation for that part. If the underlined part is correct, mark "Correct as is."**

**David has never <u>skated but he</u> wants to learn.**

**A** skated. but he

**B** skated but, he

**C** skated, but he

**D** Correct as is

**11 Choose the word that is spelled correctly and completes the sentence.**

**The car stopped at the stop ______.**

**A** sign

**B** sine

**C** sighn

**D** sien

> **Tip**
> Remember that some letters are silent. If you don't hear the sound for a letter that you see in a word, the word may still be spelled correctly.

**12 Write a sentence about a sculpture or painting you have seen. Use an irregular verb in the past tense or an irregular verb with the helping verb *have, has,* or *had.* Capitalize and punctuate correctly.**

______________________________

______________________________

______________________________



| | |
|---|---|
| 9 | Ⓐ Ⓑ Ⓒ Ⓓ |
| 10 | Ⓐ Ⓑ Ⓒ Ⓓ |
| 11 | Ⓐ Ⓑ Ⓒ Ⓓ |

STOP

Name ______________________________

## *Directions*

**Write one or more paragraphs to persuade others to visit a particular place in your community. Include reasons and details to support your ideas.**

**Use the space below to plan your writing. Then write the composition on a separate sheet of paper. Use the Writer's Checklist to revise and edit your work.**

**Tip**

This topic calls for persuasive writing. Think of a place in your community that people would enjoy visiting. Why would they enjoy it? You might organize your ideas in a web with your opinion in the center and reasons and details around it.

Name ____________________

## *Writer's Checklist*

- ❏ Be sure you stated your opinion clearly.
- ❏ Use specific reasons and details to support your opinion.
- ❏ Be sure all of your sentences relate to your topic.
- ❏ Include a variety of sentence types.
- ❏ Use interesting words and phrases.
- ❏ Use correct grammar, punctuation, capitalization, and spelling.
- ❏ Use complete sentences.
- ❏ Write clearly and neatly.

**Tip**
Begin a persuasive composition by telling readers what you think or feel about the topic and suggesting what they should do. Then give them good reasons to follow your suggestion.

**Tip**
Make sure each sentence has a subject and a verb. Does each sentence express a complete thought?





STOP

Name ____________________

*Directions*

**Read the article below. Then answer questions 1 through 5. You may look back at the article.**

# The Lewis and Clark Expedition

In his first term in office, President Thomas Jefferson nearly doubled the size of the United States in one move. He did this by buying a huge territory from the French government in what came to be called the Louisiana Purchase. The territory stretched west from the Mississippi River to the Rocky Mountains.

President Jefferson asked Meriwether Lewis to head an expedition to explore the new land. Lewis asked Lieutenant William Clark to lead it with him. Their plan was to travel by boat up the Missouri River, walk to the Columbia River, and then travel by boat again to the Pacific Ocean.

The expedition began in May of 1804. In the fall, they reached a Mandan Indian village. There they hired a French guide. His Native American wife, Sacagawea, proved to be a better guide and interpreter than her husband. She helped the explorers find their way through the unfamiliar territory.

After a year, Lewis and Clark expected to find the Columbia River. Instead, they saw only mountains stretching before them. Just when finding the river seemed hopeless, the explorers met a group of Shoshoni Indians. Sacagawea recognized one of the chiefs as her brother. He sold the group many horses and found them a new guide.

After more than two years, the explorers returned to their starting point in St. Louis, Missouri. The Lewis and Clark Expedition was one of the most important journeys ever taken in this country. Lewis and Clark helped map new territory and provided information about the people, plants, and animals that lived there.

**Tip**
If you don't recognize the word *Expedition,* continue reading to see if you can figure out the meaning from the context.

**Tip**
This article contains many facts. Read it quickly to get the main idea. You can go back later to find information to answer questions.

**Tip**
What opinion does the author express in this paragraph? What reasons are given to support that opinion?

**Lewis and Clark Expedition Time Line**

| Louisiana Purchase | Lewis and Clark begin expedition | expedition returns to St. Louis |
|---|---|---|
| 1803 | 1804 | 1806 |

Name ______________________________

**1 This article is expository nonfiction because it**

**A** presents and explains information

**B** tells a story

**C** combines elements of fiction and nonfiction

**D** is set in the past

**2 Which of these sentences expresses an opinion?**

**A** The territory stretched west from the Mississippi River to the Rocky Mountains.

**B** They saw only mountains stretching before them.

**C** The Lewis and Clark Expedition was one of the most important journeys ever taken in this country.

**D** More than two years after they began their journey, the explorers returned to their starting point in St. Louis, Missouri.

> **Tip**
> Remember that an opinion tells what someone feels or believes. The statement cannot be proved.

**3 Which of these facts supports the opinion you identified in Question 2?**

**A** The land was bought from the French government.

**B** The expedition began in May, 1804.

**C** Lewis asked Clark to lead the expedition with him.

**D** Lewis and Clark helped make maps of the new territory.

> **Tip**
> All the statements are facts. Which one states a reason that might persuade someone to agree with the opinion you identified in Question 2?

**4 What information can you learn from the time line that is *not* given in the article?**

**A** The expedition began in 1804.

**B** The journey took more than two years.

**C** The Louisiana Purchase took place in 1803.

**D** The expedition began and ended in St. Louis.

> **Tip**
> To answer this question, check both the article and the time line. Pay attention to the word *not.* It tells you that the correct answer is the information found only on the time line, not in the article.

**5 Write one or two sentences to summarize this article.**

______________________________

______________________________

______________________________

| | |
|---|---|
| 1 | Ⓐ Ⓑ Ⓒ Ⓓ |
| 2 | Ⓐ Ⓑ Ⓒ Ⓓ |
| 3 | Ⓐ Ⓑ Ⓒ Ⓓ |
| 4 | Ⓐ Ⓑ Ⓒ Ⓓ |





GO ON

Name ______________________________

*Directions*

**Read this paragraph from a report a student wrote about a surprising discovery. It has several mistakes that need correcting. Then answer Questions 6 through 8.**

| |
|---|
| [1] In 1991, two hikers on a mountain trail in northern Italy spotted something nearby. [2] It was a human body. [3] It was a hunter who has died more than 5,000 years ago. [4] Scientists hurried to the site to remove the remains and to begin studying this important find. |

**6 Where would this sentence best fit in the paragraph?**

**However, it wasn't the body of a hiker they found in the melting ice.**

**A** after Sentence 1
**B** after Sentence 2
**C** after Sentence 3
**D** after Sentence 4

> **Tip**
> At first, you might think the new sentence fits after Sentence 1, but does it really make sense there when you read the whole paragraph? The best place for the new sentence is probably somewhere else.

**7 Which is the best way to rewrite Sentence 3?**

**A** It was a hunter who had died more than 5,000 years ago.
**B** It is a hunter who has died more than 5,000 years ago.
**C** It has been a hunter who has died more than 5,000 years ago.
**D** It had been a hunter who have died more than 5,000 years ago

**8 The word *site* in Sentence 4 means**

**A** to rest on a seat
**B** ability to see
**C** place
**D** a large town

> **Tip**
> If you don't know this word, reread the sentence and use the context to figure out its meaning. Don't confuse this word with a homophone that is pronounced the same way but is spelled differently.



| | |
|---|---|
| 6 | Ⓐ Ⓑ Ⓒ Ⓓ |
| 7 | Ⓐ Ⓑ Ⓒ Ⓓ |
| 8 | Ⓐ Ⓑ Ⓒ Ⓓ |

Name ______________________________________________

*Directions*

**Look at the underlined part of the sentence. Choose the answer that shows the correct wording for that part. If the underlined part is correct, mark "Correct as is."**

**9** **He <u>didn't do none</u> of the work.**

**A** do none

**B** did not do none

**C** didn't do any

**D** Correct as is

> **Tip**
> Remember that it is an error to use two negatives in a sentence. Which answer shows how to correct this error?

**10** **Read the phrases. Look for an underlined word that contains a usage error. If all the underlined words are used correctly, mark "All correct."**

**A** Sam's and <u>our's</u>

**B** <u>we're</u> ready

**C** <u>shouldn't</u> take long

**D** All correct

> **Tip**
> Decide whether each underlined word is a contraction or a possessive pronoun. Contractions are written with apostrophes, but possessive pronouns are not.

**11** **Choose the word that is spelled correctly and completes the sentence.**

**He ______ go there often.**

**A** doesnt

**B** does'nt

**C** doesnt'

**D** doesn't

**12** **Write a sentence about exploring or explorers. Use a contraction in your sentence. Capitalize and punctuate correctly.**

______________________________________________

______________________________________________

______________________________________________

| | |
|---|---|
| 9 | Ⓐ Ⓑ Ⓒ Ⓓ |
| 10 | Ⓐ Ⓑ Ⓒ Ⓓ |
| 11 | Ⓐ Ⓑ Ⓒ Ⓓ |

STOP

Name ______________________________

*Directions*

**Read the story below. Then answer Questions 1 through 5. You may look back at the story.**

# Dancing on the Edge of the World

The first time I saw the Pacific Ocean waves crashing against the cliffs, I knew I would make this spot my home. This area of the California coast was once called *el país grande del sur*, "the big country of the south." Later, these 75 miles of rough seacoast became known simply as "Big Sur."

> **Tip**
> Notice that the story is told in the first-person. The narrator uses the pronouns *I* and *my*.

I came here in 1890 during the Big Sur Gold Rush, but I didn't come to find gold. I planned to make a living in the limestone business. The Rockland Cement Company had set up its headquarters in Limekiln Canyon in the 1880s. By the time I arrived, schooners were making frequent trips in and out of Rockland Landing. These sailing ships brought in supplies and carried away large quantities of limestone bricks.

> **Tip**
> You may not recognize the word *schooners,* but you can use word relationships to figure out its meaning.

In those days, Big Sur had few roads. Its mountains and deep canyons made travel difficult. Only 1,000 people or so lived in the region. My neighbors made their living by ranching, logging redwoods, or mining gold.

There are few beaches along the rocky Big Sur coastline. We do have beautiful mountain streams and a wide variety of plant and animal life. Mighty coast redwoods grow in the canyons. Mountain lions, deer, and many other animals and birds share the land with us.

Since I arrived fifty years ago, more settlers have come. Hotels and resorts have opened. The biggest change was the building of Highway 1. It opened three years ago, in 1937. Machines came and blasted through the cliffs. Debris damaged canyons and waterfalls. On the other hand, land is being set aside to protect the beauty of Big Sur.

Long before my time, Big Sur was the home of the Ohlone Indians. They sang a song about "dancing on the edge of the world." One can still see how the Ohlone might imagine that the beautiful but harsh landscape of Big Sur, where jagged cliffs plunge into the sea, was indeed "the edge of the world."

> **Tip**
> Why do you think the author waits until the end of the story to tell you what the title means? Were there any clues that gave you an idea about it before this?

Name ______________________________

**1 You can tell that this story is historical fiction because**

**A** it is told in the first person

**B** the characters do things that real people would not do

**C** it is set in a real time and place in the past

**D** the events are like events in real life

> **Tip**
> The correct answer names a characteristic that is true for *all* historical fiction stories and helps you tell the difference between historical fiction and other kinds of writing.

**2 You can figure out the meaning of the word *schooners* in the story from**

**A** the words *sailing ships* in the next sentence

**B** the word *headquarters* in the sentence before

**C** the words *frequent trips* in the same sentence

**D** the words *limestone bricks* in the next sentence

> **Tip**
> Scan the story to find the word *schooners*. Then reread the sentences mentioned in the answer choices.

**3 According to the story, the most important change in fifty years was**

**A** the arrival of more settlers

**B** the building of Highway 1

**C** the building of hotels and resorts

**D** damage to canyons and waterfalls

> **Tip**
> All the answer choices tell about changes mentioned in the story. The key words in the question are *most important.*

**4 The Ohlone Indians might have written the song about the "edge of the world" because**

**A** the area had such beautiful scenery

**B** they lived in a place where steep cliffs met the sea

**C** they wanted to describe the area's wildlife

**D** dancing was their favorite activity

**5 Write one or more sentences to describe how this story made you feel. What was it about the story that made you feel this way?**

______________________________

______________________________

______________________________

| | |
|---|---|
| 1 | Ⓐ Ⓑ Ⓒ Ⓓ |
| 2 | Ⓐ Ⓑ Ⓒ Ⓓ |
| 3 | Ⓐ Ⓑ Ⓒ Ⓓ |
| 4 | Ⓐ Ⓑ Ⓒ Ⓓ |

Name ______________________________

## *Directions*

**Read this paragraph from a report a student wrote about settlers on the Great Plains. It has several mistakes that need correcting. Then answer Questions 6 through 8.**

> [1] Settlers who came to make their homes on the Great Plains found rich grasslands but no trees. [2] They had no wood for building homes, so many of them building houses of sod. [3] Houses in different parts of the world are built from a variety of materials. [4] Sod is soil held together by the tangled roots of grass and weeds. [5] The settlers cut the sod into blocks and piled them in rows to build walls.

**6 Which sentence does *not* belong in the paragraph?**

**A** Sentence 2
**B** Sentence 3
**C** Sentence 4
**D** Sentence 5

> **Tip**
> First identify the topic or main idea of the paragraph. The sentence that does not belong is the one that does not tell about that topic.

**7 Which is the best way to rewrite Sentence 2?**

**A** They had no wood for building homes, so many of them build houses of sod.
**B** They had no wood for building homes, so many of them are building houses of sod.
**C** They had no wood for building homes, so many of them built houses of sod.
**D** They had no wood for building homes, so many of them has built houses of sod.

**8 Which of these resources would be most helpful in gathering information for this report?**

**A** an on-line encyclopedia article about the Great Plains
**B** a website that shows homes for sale
**C** a map of the United States that shows the Great Plains
**D** a chapter about soil in a science text

> **Tip**
> Think about the kinds of information you might find in each of the resources. Which one is most likely to give the kinds of facts used in the paragraph?



| | |
|---|---|
| 6 | Ⓐ Ⓑ Ⓒ Ⓓ |
| 7 | Ⓐ Ⓑ Ⓒ Ⓓ |
| 8 | Ⓐ Ⓑ Ⓒ Ⓓ |

Name ______________________________

## *Directions*

**Choose the word that correctly completes the sentence.**

**9 The women walked ________ down the path.**

**A** swift
**B** swifter
**C** swiftly
**D** swiftness

> **Tip**
> The word that correctly completes the sentence describes the verb *walked.* Which of the answer choices is an adverb?

**10 Which phrase is an example of alliteration?**

**A** as high as the sky
**B** under a gray rock
**C** popped up
**D** tall towering trees

**11 Read the phrases. Choose the phrase containing an underlined word that is spelled wrong. If all the underlined words are spelled correctly, mark "All correct."**

**A** a boat's white <u>sail</u>
**B** pick a purple <u>flower</u>
**C** <u>sore</u> into the sky
**D** All correct

> **Tip**
> Homophones like *sail* and *sale, flower* and *flour,* or *sore* and *soar* are easy to confuse. Is the correct word used in each of the phrases?

**12 Write a sentence about an adventure. Use at least one adverb in your sentence. Circle each adverb. Capitalize and punctuate correctly.**

______________________________________________

______________________________________________

______________________________________________



| | |
|---|---|
| 9 | Ⓐ Ⓑ Ⓒ Ⓓ |
| 10 | Ⓐ Ⓑ Ⓒ Ⓓ |
| 11 | Ⓐ Ⓑ Ⓒ Ⓓ |

STOP

Name ______________________________

*Directions*

**Read the story below. Then answer Questions 1 through 5. You may look back at the story.**

# Tony Beaver

The mountains of West Virginia were so rough and rocky that only the mightiest pioneers could settle there. Even among these pioneers, the Beaver family was unusual. Paw and Maw Beaver lived in a log cabin on top of a hill with the three little Beavers, who were named Betsey, Tony, and Molly.

Betsey and Molly were growing up big and healthy, but Tony grew so extra large that Maw sent him to strike out on his own. Tony set out, stepping from mountaintop to mountaintop, until he came to Turtle Cove. There he met Big Bill Simpson, who invited him to join a woodchopping contest.

> **Tip**
> Can anyone really step from mountaintop to mountaintop? What does this exaggeration tell you about the kind of story this might be?

Tony had chopped down trees for Paw, so he told Big Bill he'd give it a try. Ready, set, go! Tony swung his ax so hard that a huge hickory tree broke off like a matchstick. Big Bill hired Tony, and that's how Tony got into the lumbering business.

> **Tip**
> Based on what you have read so far, how do you predict Tony will do in the lumbering business?

Before long, Tony had figured out how to cut down two trees with one swing. He'd cut down one on the back swing and one on the down swing. Pretty soon he got bored with that and just started pulling trees out by the roots.

Tony Beaver was as famous a logger in West Virginia as his cousin Paul Bunyan was up north. Like Paul, who had Babe the Blue Ox, Tony had two oxen named Hannibal and Goliath.

One time, Tony challenged his cousin Paul to a skating contest. They wrapped slabs of bacon around their skates and raced back and forth, greasing their grandmaw's pancake griddle. Tony won that race, by the way.

> **Tip**
> Create a mental picture of Tony Beaver and Paul Bunyan skating on their grandmaw's griddle. How big would the griddle have to be?

Tony Beaver lived a long, successful life and had many great adventures. To this day, they still talk about Tony Beaver in the hills of West Virginia.

Name ____________________

**1 This story is an example of**

**A** a fable

**B** historical fiction

**C** a biography

**D** a tall tale

**2 One way that Tony Beaver and Paul Bunyan are alike is that**

**A** Paul is Tony's cousin

**B** they are loggers

**C** they are from West Virginia

**D** each has a blue ox named Babe

> **Tip**
> Imagine a Venn diagram. Which answer choice belongs in the center of the diagram, under the label "Both"?

**3 Which picture shows Hannibal and Goliath?**

**A** **B** **C** **D**

> **Tip**
> If you don't remember who Hannibal and Goliath were, scan the story to find their names. Then reread that part of the story.

**4 An example of an exaggeration in the story is the size of**

**A** the mountaintops

**B** Tony's ax

**C** the hickory tree

**D** Grandmaw's griddle

**5 Which statement expresses an opinion?**

**A** Tony had chopped down trees for Paw, so he told Big Bill he'd give it a try.

**B** Paw and Maw Beaver lived in a log cabin on top of a hill with the three little Beavers.

**C** Even among these pioneers, the Beaver family was unusual.

**D** To this day, they still talk about Tony Beaver in the hills of West Virginia.

> **Tip**
> The correct answer is the one that tells what someone thinks or feels. An opinion is not a fact, even if many people agree with it, because it cannot be proved.

| | |
|---|---|
| 1 | Ⓐ Ⓑ Ⓒ Ⓓ |
| 2 | Ⓐ Ⓑ Ⓒ Ⓓ |
| 3 | Ⓐ Ⓑ Ⓒ Ⓓ |
| 4 | Ⓐ Ⓑ Ⓒ Ⓓ |
| 5 | Ⓐ Ⓑ Ⓒ Ⓓ |





GO ON

Name ______________________________________________

# *Directions*

**Read this paragraph from a report a student wrote about tall tales. It has several mistakes that need correcting. Then answer Questions 6 through 8.**

## Tall Tales

[1] The first tall tales were told by pioneers who settled the west in the 1800s. [2] Without movies or TV to entertain them in the evenings, people gathered around and told funny stories. [3] Some tall tales were told about real people, such as Johnny Appleseed and Davy Crockett other characters in tall tales were fictional workers. [4] Loggers, cowboys, railroad workers, and steel workers all had there special heroes.

**6 Which sentence contains two complete thoughts and should be written as two sentences?**

**A** Sentence 1
**B** Sentence 2
**C** Sentence 3
**D** Sentence 4

> **Tip**
> Look for two sentences that should be written as separate sentences or as a compound sentence but are joined incorrectly.

**7 Which is the <u>best</u> way to rewrite Sentence 4?**

**A** Loggers, cowboys, railroad workers, and steel workers all had their special heroes.
**B** Loggers, cowboys, railroad workers, and steel workers all had they special heroes.
**C** Loggers, cowboys, railroad workers, and steel workers all had them special heroes.
**D** Loggers, cowboys, railroad workers, and steel workers all had they're special heroes.

> **Tip**
> Read Sentence 4 to identify the error and think of how to correct it. Then pick the answer choice that shows the correct word to replace the word *there.*

**8 What is the student's purpose for writing this report?**

**A** to entertain readers with a tall tale
**B** to persuade readers to tell tall tales
**C** to tell how to make up a tall tale
**D** to explain how tall tales began



| | |
|---|---|
| 6 | Ⓐ Ⓑ Ⓒ Ⓓ |
| 7 | Ⓐ Ⓑ Ⓒ Ⓓ |
| 8 | Ⓐ Ⓑ Ⓒ Ⓓ |

Name ____________________________________________

## *Directions*

**Choose the word or words that correctly complete the sentence.**

**9 Charlie skates ______ than I do.**

**A** faster

**B** more faster

**C** more fast

**D** most faster

> **Tip**
> When comparing two actions, add *-er* to most short adverbs. Use *more* before most adverbs of two or more syllables.

**10 Choose the words that correctly complete the sentence.**

**The large bell ______ , but the small bell ______.**

**A** thudded, banged

**B** chattered, boomed

**C** clanged, jingled

**D** buzzed, snapped

> **Tip**
> All the answer choices are examples of onomatopoeia, or words that imitate sounds. Pick the two sounds that make sense in the context of the sentence.

**11 Read the phrases. Choose the phrase containing an underlined word that is spelled wrong. If all the underlined words are spelled correctly, mark "All correct."**

**A** <u>carrot</u> seeds

**B** <u>spilled</u> milk

**C** deliver a <u>package</u>

**D** All correct

**12 Write a sentence about an imaginary hero. Use an adverb to compare two actions or to compare three or more actions. Capitalize and punctuate correctly.**

____________________________________________

____________________________________________

____________________________________________



| | |
|---|---|
| 9 | Ⓐ Ⓑ Ⓒ Ⓓ |
| 10 | Ⓐ Ⓑ Ⓒ Ⓓ |
| 11 | Ⓐ Ⓑ Ⓒ Ⓓ |

STOP

Name ______________________________

# *Directions*

**Read the poem below. Then answer Questions 1 through 5. You may look back at the poem.**

## Lizards

Lizards are shy. In fact, most are meek.
Lizards are small, swift, smooth, and sleek.
Whether they're orange, blue, yellow, or green,
Lizards, I think, prefer not to be seen.
Quick as a sneeze, they scurry from sight.
It doesn't take much to give them a fright!
They hide in dark corners where no one can see them,
Although there are some that live in museums.
Even in cages, they hide from our view.
Are you scared of lizards? They're frightened of you!

**Tip**
As you read, look for words that help you create a mental picture of lizards and how they behave.

Name ______________________________

1 **Which of these statements is <u>not</u> true about the poem?**

**A** Each verse has two lines that rhyme.

**B** It uses alliteration, or words with similar beginning sounds.

**C** The tone of the poem is dark and gloomy.

**D** It contains many adjectives that tell about lizards.

> **Tip**
> Pay attention to the key word *not*. Three of the statements are true about the poem. To answer the question, find the one statements that is *not* true.

2 **Two words in the poem that are synonyms are**

**A** *small* and *swift*

**B** *hide* and *dark*

**C** *blue* and *yellow*

**D** *shy* and *meek*

> **Tip**
> Remember that synonyms are words that have the same or similar meanings.

3 **What does the poem mean when it says "Quick as a sneeze, they scurry from sight"?**

**A** Lizards are frightened by sneezes.

**B** Lizards run and hide in as little time as it takes to sneeze.

**C** Sneezing helps lizards run faster.

**D** Lizards make a sneezing sound to warn each other of danger.

4 **Which statement best expresses the poet's opinion?**

**A** People should not be afraid of lizards.

**B** Lizards make great pets.

**C** People and lizards are alike in many ways.

**D** Lizards are scary creatures.

5 **Write one or more sentences to tell how this poem makes you feel.**

______________________________

______________________________

______________________________

> **Tip**
> The question asks you to write about your feelings. For example, you might tell about feelings you had as you read the poem or how you feel about lizards as a result of reading the poem.



| | |
|---|---|
| 1 | Ⓐ Ⓑ Ⓒ Ⓓ |
| 2 | Ⓐ Ⓑ Ⓒ Ⓓ |
| 3 | Ⓐ Ⓑ Ⓒ Ⓓ |
| 4 | Ⓐ Ⓑ Ⓒ Ⓓ |

Name ______________________________

*Directions*

**Read this paragraph that a student wrote about a helicopter ride. It has several mistakes that need correcting. Then answer Questions 6 through 8.**

[1] Today Demitri had a truly unforgettable experience—an exciting helicopter ride. [2] After the helicopter landed, the passengers strolled among spectacular gardens. [3] The fragrance of the flowers fills the air. [4] From the helicopter, Demitri could see green valleys, soaring cliffs, and tumbling mountain waterfalls.

**6 How should the sentences in the paragraph be organized?**

**A** 1, 2, 3, 4

**B** 1, 4, 2, 3

**C** 1, 2, 4, 3

**D** 1, 3, 2, 4

> **Tip**
> Rearrange and reread the sentences according to each answer choice to see which one makes sense and tells events in a logical order.

**7 Which is the best way to rewrite Sentence 3?**

**A** The fragrance of the flowers fill the air.

**B** The fragrance of the flowers filling the air.

**C** The fragrance of the flowers filled the air.

**D** The fragrance of the flowers has filled the air.

> **Tip**
> Think about the tense in which the rest of the paragraph is written to choose the correct tense of the verb.

**8 A compound word used in this paragraph is**

**A** waterfalls

**B** spectacular

**C** unforgettable

**D** passengers



| | |
|---|---|
| 6 | Ⓐ Ⓑ Ⓒ Ⓓ |
| 7 | Ⓐ Ⓑ Ⓒ Ⓓ |
| 8 | Ⓐ Ⓑ Ⓒ Ⓓ |

Name ___________________________________________

## *Directions*

**Look at the underlined part of the sentence. Choose the answer that shows the correct capitalization for that part. If the underlined part is correct, mark "Correct as is."**

**9 "<u>Strange Plants Of the Rain Forest"</u> is the name of a magazine article I'm reading.**

- **A** "Strange plants of the Rain Forest"
- **B** "Strange Plants Of The Rain Forest"
- **C** "Strange Plants of the Rain Forest"
- **D** Correct as is

> **Tip**
> Take time to look carefully at the title. Be sure that each word that needs to be capitalized is capitalized in your answer choice.

**10 Choose the word that correctly completes the sentence.**

**Please sit beside _______.**

- **A** I
- **B** me
- **C** myself
- **D** my

> **Tip**
> The word *beside* is a preposition. What form of the pronoun should follow the preposition?

**11 Choose the word that is spelled correctly and completes the sentence.**

**Mom said this was her ______ warning to clean my room.**

- **A** finnal
- **B** finell
- **C** finale
- **D** final

**12 Write a sentence about a good hiding place for a small animal or other creature. Use a preposition in your sentence. Write P above the preposition and O above the object of the preposition. Capitalize and punctuate correctly.**

_______________________________________________

_______________________________________________

_______________________________________________

| | |
|---|---|
| 9 | Ⓐ Ⓑ Ⓒ Ⓓ |
| 10 | Ⓐ Ⓑ Ⓒ Ⓓ |
| 11 | Ⓐ Ⓑ Ⓒ Ⓓ |

STOP

Name ______________________________

*Directions*

**Read the story below. Then answer Questions 1 through 5. You may look back at the story.**

# Visiting the Online Museum

Nira frowned at the computer screen and sighed. Her brother Miko sighed, too. He loved using the computer, but it was Nira's turn. He was trying to read his history lesson while he waited, but it wasn't easy. Nira sighed again, louder this time.

> **Tip**
> Pay attention to how Nira acts. What do her actions tell you about how she is feeling?

"Okay, what is it?" Miko asked.

"We're supposed to go to a museum this weekend and write a report about it," Nira said. "I can't go Saturday because of my soccer game. I was doing a search for a museum that's open on Sunday, but I can't find one. So I don't know what to do."

> **Tip**
> In this paragraph, Nira explains her problem. You need to identify the problem in a story in order to understand the plot.

Miko said, "I know what you can do, but you have to let me get on the computer."

> **Tip**
> As you read, make predictions about what might happen next. Do you think Miko will help Nira? What do you think he may do?

"It's my turn, though," Nira complained.

"Come on!" Miko insisted. "You don't even like using the computer."

"Well, all right," Nira said. "It just takes so long." She slid over and let Miko sit at the keyboard. He made a few clicks with the mouse and then turned the monitor so that it faced her.

"There," he said. A brightly-colored picture of a Sioux chief filled the screen. Next to the picture was information about the painter and the painting. "It's the art museum in the city," Miko said. "You can find all sorts of information, paintings, and items from all the collections."

"Is it really the museum?" Nira asked.

"Sure it is," Miko said. "Part of the exhibit is online. Have fun, click with the mouse, and look around. Don't worry. You'll be able to write the best report in class. You might even get extra credit for being the only student to visit an online museum!"

Name ______________________________

**1 At the beginning of the story, Nira feels**

**A** delighted

**B** annoyed

**C** sorrowful

**D** hopeful

> **Tip**
> The story does not say how Nira feels, but you can figure it out from her actions at the beginning of the story and from your own experience.

**2 In the phrases *Nira's turn* and *turned the monitor*, the words *turn* and *turned***

**A** have the same meaning

**B** are different parts of speech with different meanings

**C** are verbs written in two different tenses

**D** are nouns that have different meanings

**3 In addition to the main purpose of entertaining readers, the author may also have wanted to**

**A** give directions for doing a computer search

**B** give information about museums

**C** advertise the online museum

**D** persuade readers to take advantage of online resources

**4 Which sentence best expresses the author's perspective?**

**A** Online museums are better than real ones.

**B** Students should spend less time on the computer.

**C** The computer can be a helpful tool for students.

**D** Visiting museums is a waste of time.

> **Tip**
> The author's perspective is his or her opinion about a subject. Determine the author's perspective by thinking about the details and language he or she used in the story.

**5 Write one or more sentences to identify the problem Nira has in the story and tell how is it resolved.**

______________________________

______________________________

______________________________

______________________________



| | |
|---|---|
| 1 | Ⓐ Ⓑ Ⓒ Ⓓ |
| 2 | Ⓐ Ⓑ Ⓒ Ⓓ |
| 3 | Ⓐ Ⓑ Ⓒ Ⓓ |
| 4 | Ⓐ Ⓑ Ⓒ Ⓓ |

Name ____________________

# *Directions*

**Read this topic sentence that a student wrote for the first draft of a report on a famous museum. Then answer questions 6 through 8.**

***When architect Frank Lloyd Wright designed the building that would hold the Guggenheim Museum, he looked to nature.***

**6 Choose the sentences that best develop the topic sentence.**

**A** A recent exhibit on motorcycles was especially popular. Millions of visitors flocked to the museum to see it.

**B** The museum resembles the spiral shell of a sea animal called the nautilus. The main exhibition hall is built in the shape of a spiral.

**C** The Guggenheim museum is located in New York City. It opened in 1959.

**D** Frank Lloyd Wright designed other famous buildings, too. He is regarded as one of the outstanding architects of his time.

> **Tip**
> All of the choices tell something about the Guggenheim Museum or about Frank Lloyd Wright. The correct choice is the detail that gives more information about the main idea expressed in the topic sentence.

**7 What is the <u>best</u> pattern to use for organizing the paragraph?**

**A** cause and effect

**B** compare and contrast

**C** main idea and details

**D** sequence

> **Tip**
> Reread the topic sentence and the sentences you chose as your answer for Question 6. What pattern or text structure do you recognize?

**8 For what purpose would this report be written?**

**A** to entertain readers with an interesting story

**B** to give information about the life of Frank Lloyd Wright

**C** to describe the structure of the Guggenheim Museum

**D** to persuade readers to visit the museum



| | |
|---|---|
| 6 | Ⓐ Ⓑ Ⓒ Ⓓ |
| 7 | Ⓐ Ⓑ Ⓒ Ⓓ |
| 8 | Ⓐ Ⓑ Ⓒ Ⓓ |

Name ______________________________

*Directions*

**Look at the underlined part of the sentence. Choose the answer that correctly describes the underlined part.**

**9** **You can see many beautiful paintings and other interesting items at our local art museum.**

**A** an independent clause

**B** a dependent clause

**C** a prepositional phrase

**D** a compound predicate

**Tip**
Remember that clauses and predicates contain verbs. A prepositional phrase contains a preposition but no verb. Can you find a verb in the underlined part of the sentence? Can you find a preposition?

**10** **Choose the word that correctly completes the sentence.**

**The little striped kitten is the ______ of them all.**

**A** cuter

**B** more cute

**C** cutest

**D** most cutest

**11** **Read the phrases. Choose the phrase containing an underlined word that is spelled wrong. If all the underlined words are spelled correctly, mark "All correct."**

**A** an enormous box

**B** a poppular song

**C** a herd of elephants

**D** All correct

**12** **Write a sentence about a homework assignment that you found especially challenging or interesting. Include a prepositional phrase in your sentence. Capitalize and punctuate correctly.**

**Tip**
Remember that a prepositional phrase consists of a preposition and the object of the preposition, and may also include other words in between.

______________________________

______________________________

______________________________

| | |
|---|---|
| 9 | Ⓐ Ⓑ Ⓒ Ⓓ |
| 10 | Ⓐ Ⓑ Ⓒ Ⓓ |
| 11 | Ⓐ Ⓑ Ⓒ Ⓓ |

STOP

Name ____________________

## *Directions*

**Write one or more paragraphs about why it is important to follow directions. Include examples to make your point clear.**

**Use the space below to plan your writing. Then write the composition on a separate sheet of paper. Use the Writer's Checklist to revise and edit your work.**

**Tip**

This topic calls for informative writing. Think of times when it is important to follow directions. Why is it important? An outline might be useful to organize your thoughts.





GO ON

Name ______________________________

## *Writer's Checklist*

- ❏ Be sure you wrote about why it is important to follow directions.
- ❏ Use specific details to support your response.
- ❏ Include a variety of sentence types.
- ❏ Use interesting words and phrases.
- ❏ Organize your response in a clear and logical way.
- ❏ Use correct punctuation, capitalization, and spelling.
- ❏ Use complete sentences.
- ❏ Write clearly and neatly.

**Tip**
Answering the prompt is the most important part of a writing test. Make sure that you have done what the prompt is asking.

**Tip**
You can vary your sentences by combining some shorter sentences into compound or complex sentences. You can also add variety by using prepositional phrases.





STOP

Name ______________________________

## Practice Test
## Answer Sheet

### Reading

Sample

1 Ⓐ ● Ⓒ Ⓓ

Sample

2 Ⓐ Ⓑ Ⓒ Ⓓ

1 Ⓐ Ⓑ Ⓒ Ⓓ
2 Ⓐ Ⓑ Ⓒ Ⓓ
3 Ⓐ Ⓑ Ⓒ Ⓓ
4
5 Ⓐ Ⓑ Ⓒ Ⓓ
6 Ⓐ Ⓑ Ⓒ Ⓓ
7 Ⓐ Ⓑ Ⓒ Ⓓ
8 Ⓐ Ⓑ Ⓒ Ⓓ
9 Ⓐ Ⓑ Ⓒ Ⓓ
10 Ⓐ Ⓑ Ⓒ Ⓓ
11 Ⓐ Ⓑ Ⓒ Ⓓ
12
13 Ⓐ Ⓑ Ⓒ Ⓓ
14 Ⓐ Ⓑ Ⓒ Ⓓ
15 Ⓐ Ⓑ Ⓒ Ⓓ
16 Ⓐ Ⓑ Ⓒ Ⓓ
17 Ⓐ Ⓑ Ⓒ Ⓓ
18 Ⓐ Ⓑ Ⓒ Ⓓ

### Language Arts

Sample

1 Ⓐ Ⓑ Ⓒ ●

Sample

2 Ⓐ Ⓑ Ⓒ Ⓓ

1 Ⓐ Ⓑ Ⓒ Ⓓ
2 Ⓐ Ⓑ Ⓒ Ⓓ
3 Ⓐ Ⓑ Ⓒ Ⓓ
4 Ⓐ Ⓑ Ⓒ Ⓓ
5 Ⓐ Ⓑ Ⓒ Ⓓ
6 Ⓐ Ⓑ Ⓒ Ⓓ
7 Ⓐ Ⓑ Ⓒ Ⓓ
8 Ⓐ Ⓑ Ⓒ Ⓓ
9 Ⓐ Ⓑ Ⓒ Ⓓ
10 Ⓐ Ⓑ Ⓒ Ⓓ
11 Ⓐ Ⓑ Ⓒ Ⓓ
12 Ⓐ Ⓑ Ⓒ Ⓓ
13
14 Ⓐ Ⓑ Ⓒ Ⓓ
15 Ⓐ Ⓑ Ⓒ Ⓓ
16 Ⓐ Ⓑ Ⓒ Ⓓ
17
18 Ⓐ Ⓑ Ⓒ Ⓓ
19 Ⓐ Ⓑ Ⓒ Ⓓ
20 Ⓐ Ⓑ Ⓒ Ⓓ
21
22 Ⓐ Ⓑ Ⓒ Ⓓ
23 Ⓐ Ⓑ Ⓒ Ⓓ
24 Ⓐ Ⓑ Ⓒ Ⓓ
25





GO ON

Name ______________________________

*Directions*

**Read each selection and the questions that follow it. Choose the best answer for each question. The correct answer for Sample 1 has been marked to show you how to mark your answers. Mark your answer for Sample 2.**

### Sample Selection

## Making Beads

It is easy and fun to create your own beads. You need glue, a pencil, and brightly-colored magazine pages. First, cut the pages into inch-wide strips. Then spread the glue on one strip. Next, fold one end of the strip around the pencil and gently roll it into a tight tube. Last, remove the pencil and let the glue dry. Follow the same steps with the other strips. When all the beads have dried, string them on wire or strong string.

**Sample 1**

**The purpose of this passage is to**

**A** invite you to an exhibit of handmade beads

**(B)** tell you how to make beads from paper

**C** describe the kinds of paper you can use to make beads

**D** persuade you to make your own beads instead of buying them

**Sample 2**

**The passage is organized according to**

**A** main idea and details

**B** compare and contrast

**C** sequence

**D** cause and effect

Name ____________________

**Trying Out**

"Are you sure you want to do this?" Sophia's mother asked as she stopped in front of the Jackson Heights Athletic Field. "You've never tried out for any kind of team before."

"I know," Sophia said, "but I want to try." She waved good-bye to her mother and walked toward the field. She was feeling a little bit nervous.

As she looked around, she saw many girls. Some looked older, and others looked about her own age. Some of the girls had their own soccer balls. Sophia hadn't known that she was supposed to bring one. She began to worry. The other girls all looked like they knew what they were doing. She felt as though she must be the only one who was trying out for the first time.

After thirty minutes of practice, Sophia's name was called. The woman running the tryouts told Sophia that most of the girls who were there had played on teams before. Sophia handed her permission slip to the woman and started to kick the ball. When she had finished, the woman thanked her. Then Sophia went back to the sidelines.

One by one, all the girls finished their tryouts and left. Soon, Sophia was the only girl still there. The woman came and asked her, "Isn't someone coming to get you?"

"My mother will be here soon," Sophia told her.

The woman smiled. "You are very patient to be able to wait so long. That's good." Then she went to talk to the other coaches.

Just as Sophia's mother arrived, the woman came back with a list of the girls who had made the team. Sophia ran her finger down the list and found her name. "Thank you!" she cried. "I didn't think I'd make it. So many talented girls were trying out."

"I saw many talented girls today," the woman said, "but I was more pleased to see one very patient girl."

Name ______________________________

1 **The setting of this story is**

A an athletic field

B Sophia's school

C a sporting goods store

D Sophia's home

2 **Sophia probably wants to try out because**

A she is sure she'll make the team

B she enjoys going to tryouts

C she likes to play soccer

D many of her friends are on the team

3 **Which word does <u>not</u> describe Sophia's feelings during the events in the story?**

A worried

B jealous

C surprised

D nervous

4 **Here are some events from the story. Place the events in order from 1 to 4 by writing the numbers in the boxes next to each sentence.**

☐ Sophia goes back to the sidelines.

☐ Sophia's name is called to try out.

☐ Sophia finds her name on the list of girls who made the team.

☐ Sophia tells the woman her mother will be there soon.

5 **Which statement <u>best</u> expresses the author's perspective?**

A Girls are better soccer players than boys.

B Soccer is a challenging game.

C Tryouts should be fun for everyone.

D It is good to be patient.

6 **At the end of the story, Sophia probably feels**

A excited

B bored

C patient

D alarmed

Name ______________________________

## Comic Strips

When people open their newspapers in the morning, many of them read the comics first. Do you know why? Maybe they want to start their day with a smile.

What is a comic strip? In comics, an artist uses pictures and words to send readers a message. Early comics, or cartoons, were single pictures with few words. They mostly poked fun at people. In the early 1800s, a Japanese artist, Katsushika Hokusai, drew a cartoon of acrobats. They are doing exercises, but they look as if they are tying themselves in knots.

Most comic strips consist of three or four pictures in a row. Each picture tells you part of what is happening, with the events shown in time order from left to right. The dialogue is usually written in balloons to show which character is speaking. You have to read the dialogue and look at the pictures to understand what is going on in the story.

There are many kinds of comic strips. Some are funny, while others are designed to send messages about family life or other serious matters. Some tell stories that go on from one strip to the next.

Cartoonists have different styles. Some do simple line drawings, while others add more details or draw in a more realistic style. Some use lots of color, while others use little. The next time you look at comic strips, notice how different they are from each other. What comic strip artists all have in common is the ability to draw pictures and tell a story.

**History of Early Comic Strips**

| 1895 | 1919 | 1931 |
|---|---|---|
| "The Yellow Kid" by R.F. Outcault; the first popular color comic | "Popeye" by E.C. Segar; Popeye, Olive Oyl, and Wimpy are well known even today | "Dick Travy" by Chester Gould; the first comic strip that wasn't funny |

Name ______________________________

**7 This article is mostly about**

**A** comic strips of the past and today

**B** the first comic strip

**C** different drawing styles of comic strip artists

**D** why people like comic strips

**8 Comic strips are stories that**

**A** never use words

**B** are always funny

**C** are told with words and pictures

**D** poke fun at people

**9 In this article, the word *dialogue* means**

**A** drawings of balloons

**B** funny drawings of acrobats

**C** message

**D** words said by characters

**10 According to the time line, the first popular color comic strip was**

**A** about acrobats

**B** "The Yellow Kid"

**C** "Popeye"

**D** not funny

**11 The comic strip "Popeye" was drawn by**

**A** Katsushika Hokusai

**B** R.F. Outcault

**C** Chester Gould

**D** E.C. Segar

**12 Write one or more sentences to summarize this article.**

______________________________

______________________________

______________________________

______________________________





GO ON

Name ______________________________

## The Stonecutter

### A Japanese Folktale

Once there was a stonecutter who was content with his life. Then one day he saw a splendid home. "I wish I had a home like this!" he cried.

When the stonecutter got home, his little house was gone. In its place stood a huge palace. The stonecutter was delighted. Soon, however, summer came. The sun burned hotter and hotter in the sky each day. Even in his fine palace, the stonecutter could not stand the heat. At last he cried out, "I am rich, but the sun is more powerful. I wish I were the sun!"

Now the stonecutter became the sun. He felt mighty and powerful. He shined his rays on the earth until the rice crops and flowers dried up in the fields, and he burned the faces of poor folk and rich folk alike.

Then one day a cloud covered the face of the sun. The sun cried out, "I am powerful, but this cloud is mightier. I wish I were a cloud!"

So the stonecutter became a cloud. He rained on the earth, and it grew green again. He poured down rain until rivers overflowed, and floods destroyed rice fields, cities, and villages. Only the great mountain stood firm and strong.

Seeing this, the cloud cried out, "I am powerful, but the mountain is mightier. I wish I were the mountain!"

Now the stonecutter became the mountain. He stood tall and proud, not bothered by sun or rain. Then one day he heard a noise. A stonecutter was striking his surface with tools. A great block of stone broke off and fell to the ground.

In anger, the mountain cried, "Is this small man mightier than I? I wish I were a man!"

So the stonecutter became a man again, in his little house. Never again did he wish to be someone or something he wasn't.

Name ___________________________________________

**13** **The second line of the title, "A Japanese Folktale," tells you that**

**A** events in the story are like events in real life

**B** the story presents facts and information

**C** the story is set in Japan at a real time in the past

**D** the story reflects the customs and beliefs of a culture

**14** **At first, the stonecutter likes being the sun because he**

**A** has a fine palace

**B** feels powerful

**C** can make the crops grow

**D** enjoys the summer heat

**15** **The stonecutter doesn't want to be the sun any more because**

**A** a cloud covers his face

**B** the rice crops dry up

**C** he can't stand the heat

**D** he would rather have a big house

**16** **Which picture shows what the rain cannot destroy?**

**A**

**B**

**C**

**D**

**17** **The only thing more powerful than the mountain is**

**A** the sun

**B** the rain

**C** floods

**D** a man

**18** **What lesson does this folktale teach?**

**A** Be happy with what you have and who you are.

**B** The more power you have, the happier you will be.

**C** It is foolish to wish for things.

**D** A true friend will always tell you the truth.

STOP

Name ______________________________

## Directions

**Look at the sample items that follow. These items will show you what the questions in the test are like and how to fill in your answers on your answer sheet. The correct answer for Sample 1 has been marked for you. Mark your answer for Sample 2.**

### Sample 1

**Choose the word that correctly completes the sentence.**

**He has _________ a lot of work today.**

**A** did

**B** do

**C** doing

**(D)** done

### Sample 2

**Look at the underlined part of the sentence. Choose the answer that shows the correct punctuation and capitalization for that part. If the underlined part is correct, mark "Correct as is."**

**Our class took a trip to the newspaper <u>office, it</u> was interesting.**

**A** office it

**B** office. It

**C** office. it

**D** office, It





STOP

Name ___________________________________________

# *Directions*

**Read this paragraph from a report a student wrote for a project on health. It has several mistakes that need correcting. Then answer Questions 1 through 3.**

> [1] People have been trying to take care of their teeth for thousands of years. [2] Gold toothpicks that are more than 5,000 years old have been found in ancient places in the Middle East. [3] Gold jewelry and other items made of gold have also been found in many places. [4] In the eighteenth century, toothbrushes were made from twigs plant roots or animal hairs. [5]The kind of toothbrush we use now wasn't invented until 1938.

**1 Which sentence does not belong in this paragraph?**

**A** Sentence 2

**B** Sentence 3

**C** Sentence 4

**D** Sentence 5

**2 Which is the <u>best</u> way to rewrite Sentence 4?**

**A** In the eighteenth century toothbrushes were made from twigs plant roots or animal hairs.

**B** In the eighteenth century toothbrushes, were made from, twigs plant roots or animal hairs.

**C** In the eighteenth century, toothbrushes were made from twigs, plant roots, or animal hairs.

**D** In the eighteenth century, toothbrushes were made from twigs, plant roots or, animal hairs.

**3 For what purpose was this report written?**

**A** to inform readers about the history of dental care

**B** to describe a gold toothpick

**C** to persuade readers to take care of their teeth

**D** to entertain readers with an amusing story

**Name** ______________________________

## *Directions*

**Read this paragraph from a report a student wrote about a person in history. It has several mistakes that need correcting. Then answer Questions 4 through 6.**

**Beau Brummell**

[1] George Bryan Brummell, known as Beau, was born in London, England, in 1778. [2] He became famous for being well dressed he wore a neckcloth called a cravat, similar to a necktie, around his neck. [3] Sometimes it taken him an entire morning to tie it perfectly. [4] Beau Brummell's clothes were so fine that even today you can find his name in the dictionary. A "Beau Brummell" is a dandy, or someone who dresses with style.

**4 Which sentence contains two complete thoughts and should be written as two sentences?**

**A** Sentence 1

**B** Sentence 2

**C** Sentence 3

**D** Sentence 4

**5 Which is the best way to rewrite Sentence 3?**

**A** Sometimes it has taken him an entire morning to tie it perfectly.

**B** Sometimes it takes him an entire morning to tie it perfectly.

**C** Sometimes it taken him an entire morning to tie it perfectly.

**D** Sometimes it took him an entire morning to tie it perfectly.

**6 Which of these resources would be most helpful in gathering information for this report?**

**A** a dictionary

**B** a book about the history of words

**C** a magazine article about the latest clothing styles

**D** an encyclopedia article about England

Name ________________________________________

## *Directions*

**Look at these parts of a letter from a fourth grade class. For Questions 7 through 9, choose the answer with the correct capitalization and punctuation.**

> North Street School
> 85 Baxter Ave.
> Gulfport, MS
>
> ____**(7)**____
>
> ____**(8)**____
>
> All the students in our class want to thank you for letting us visit the newspaper office. We enjoyed seeing the equipment and meeting the people who put out our paper every day.
>
> ____**(9)**____
>
> Ms. Amaya's Fourth Grade Class

**7** **A** June 4, 2003
**B** june 4, 2003
**C** June, 4, 2003
**D** june 4 2003

**8** **A** Dear mr Winslow,
**B** Dear Mr. Winslow
**C** Dear Mr Winslow.
**D** Dear Mr. Winslow,

**9** **A** sincerely,
**B** Sincerely,
**C** Sincerely.
**D** sincerely

Name ____________________

**10** **Choose the word or words that correctly complete the sentence.**

**Allie and her friend ________ working in the garden.**

**A** enjoy
**B** enjoys
**C** enjoying
**D** have enjoy

**11** **Look at the underlined part of the sentence. Choose the answer that shows the correct punctuation for that part. If the underlined part is correct, mark "Correct as is."**

**James got his homework done <u>early and then</u> he watched the baseball game.**

**A** early and, then
**B** early and then,
**C** early, and then
**D** Correct as is

**12** **Choose the word that is spelled correctly and completes the sentence.**

**Jan puts away the eggs and never ________ any.**

**A** brakes
**B** breakes
**C** braiks
**D** breaks

**13** **Write a complex sentence about being a good friend. Capitalize and punctuate correctly.**

______________________________

______________________________





GO ON

Name ________________________________________

**14** **Choose the word that correctly completes the sentence.**

**I like these cookies because ________ soft and chewy.**

**A** their
**B** there
**C** they're
**D** they

**15** **Which word <u>best</u> completes the analogy?**

***Cat* is to *kitten* as *hen* is to ________ .**

**A** *rooster*
**B** *duck*
**C** *flock*
**D** *chick*

**16** **Read the phrases. Look for an underlined word that contains a usage error. If all the underlined words are used correctly, mark "All correct."**

**A** the <u>bare</u> branches
**B** clear <u>blew</u> sky
**C** <u>sent</u> a letter
**D** All correct

**17** **Write a sentence in the future tense about an event that is coming up at school or at home. Capitalize and punctuate correctly.**

________________________________________

________________________________________





GO ON

Name ______________________________

**18** **Look at the underlined part of the sentence. Choose the answer that shows the correct punctuation and capitalization for that part. If the underlined part is correct, mark "Correct as is."**

**"Would you like a <u>sandwich," mom</u> asked.**

**A** sandwich?" Mom
**B** sandwich?" mom
**C** sandwich. Mom
**D** Correct as is

**19** **Read the phrases. Choose the phrase containing an underlined word that is spelled wrong. If all the underlined words are spelled correctly, mark "All correct."**

**A** a <u>mighty</u> roar
**B** at the <u>bottem</u>
**C** send a <u>message</u>
**D** Correct as is

**20** **Choose the word that correctly completes the sentence.**

**Carefully, she placed the _________ baby bird back in its nest.**

**A** helpfully
**B** helper
**C** unhelpful
**D** helpless

**21** **Write a sentence with a compound predicate to tell about two or more things your teacher does to help you learn. Capitalize and punctuate correctly.**

______________________________

______________________________

______________________________

Name ______________________________

**22** **Choose the word that is spelled correctly and completes the sentence.**

**Allen has a great __________ of baseball cards.**

**A** collecshun
**B** collectsion
**C** collection
**D** colleckson

**23** **Choose the sentences that best develop the topic sentence.**

***The kiwi cannot fly and does not look much like a bird.***

**A** Its brown fur looks like a mouse's coat. It has whiskers like a cat.
**B** Penguins can't fly, either. Penguins are found in Antarctica.
**C** There is also a fruit called the kiwi fruit. It is about the size of a plum.
**D** A type of weasel was feeding on kiwi chicks. The kiwi was in danger of disappearing.

**24** **Choose the word or words that correctly complete the sentence.**

**These shoes fit __________ than the other ones.**

**A** more good
**B** gooder
**C** more better
**D** better

**25** **Write a sentence in the present tense about your favorite story character. Then write the same sentence with the verb in the past tense.**

______________________________

______________________________

______________________________

______________________________



STOP